英语学科核心
素养发展丛书
教师系列

U0603307

落实学科核心素养在课堂

高中英语写作教学

何亚男 应晓球 主编

上海教育出版社
SHANGHAI EDUCATIONAL
PUBLISHING HOUSE

图书在版编目（CIP）数据

落实学科核心素养在课堂.高中英语写作教学／何
亚男，应晓球主编.—上海：上海教育出版社，
2020.10（2022.6重印）
ISBN 978-7-5720-0395-0

Ⅰ.①落… Ⅱ.①何… ②应… Ⅲ.①英语—写作—
教学研究—高中 Ⅳ.①G633.412

中国版本图书馆CIP数据核字（2020）第192867号

责任编辑　黄　艳　任慧子
封面设计　静斓工作室

落实学科核心素养在课堂·高中英语写作教学
何亚男　应晓球　主　编

出版发行　上海教育出版社有限公司
官　　网　www.seph.com.cn
地　　址　上海市闵行区号景路159弄C座
邮　　编　201101
印　　刷　上海展强印刷有限公司
开　　本　700×1000　1/16　印张 12.5
字　　数　205千字
版　　次　2021年1月第1版
印　　次　2022年6月第2次印刷
书　　号　ISBN 978-7-5720-0395-0/G·0288
定　　价　49.80元

如发现质量问题，读者可向本社调换　电话：021-64373213

本书编著者名单

吴彩霞　张育青　孟　莎　林　泓　施　翎
顾　欢　楼　蕾　沈珊红　沈　柳　史海蓉
姜振骅　徐　迪　徐宇琴　黄岳辉　汤　华
吴　玮　张　芸　张珏恩　周　杰　周惠英
褚朝慧　汤晓华　黄　雷　金　敏　王慧敏
陈德江　肖　丹　蔡东慧　陆永梅

本书编著者名单

吴彩霞　张育青　孟　莎　林　泓　施　翎
顾　欢　楼　蕾　沈珊红　沈　柳　史海蓉
姜振骅　徐　迪　徐宇琴　黄岳辉　汤　华
吴　玮　张　芸　张珏恩　周　杰　周惠英
储朝慧　汤晓华　黄　雷　金　敏　王慧敏
陈德江　肖　丹　蔡东慧　陆永梅

丛书序

由何亚男、应晓球、张育青、吴彩霞和金怡主持的一至三期英语学科名师培养基地为上海的英语学科建设做出了杰出的贡献，这是我们每一位上海英语教师的心声。基地编写的"高中英语课堂教学设计"丛书（包括《高中英语阅读教学设计》《高中英语语法教学活动设计》《高中英语词汇教学活动设计》和《高中英语写作教学设计》）是一套在上海普及度最广的基础教育英语教学教研丛书，十年来一直是教师们案头必备的教学设计参考书。今天我看到了这套书的全新面貌，即在《普通高中英语课程标准（2017年版2020年修订）》的理念下所做的修订版，在核心素养的背景下引领教师们实战课堂再出发。

一套书在教育教学改革的浪潮中历经十年后能够再修订，说明有很好的基础；能够被改写，说明有新的发展；能够被精简，说明编写团队提升了研究水平。在本套丛书的前言中，编委会介绍了此次修订的思想、方法和重点，以学科育人为宗旨，以培育语言能力、文化意识、思维品质和学习能力为根本，以学习活动为抓手。丛书将新课标理念、教学理论和阅读、语法、词汇、写作等教学设计紧密联系，促使教师重新审视课堂，为学生提供更丰富的语言体验和实践经历，培养学生英语学习的关键能力和必备品格。

书稿付梓，马上又要出现在我们的案头了，我们要用好这套书，上好每一节课，体现课型特征和教学结构，回报编写者在长期的实践和研究中付出的艰辛努力。首先，我们要在单元中建立语篇、词汇、语法和写作的关系，让高品质的输入保障学生个性化的输出，这样的教学才算真正领悟书中呈现给我们的教学方法，在课堂中把培育学科核心素养落到实处。同时，我们要充分利用本书中的案例开展教研活动，尤其在高中英语新教材推广使用的时候，通过深度解读案例，进行创造性实践研究，鼓励教师开展独立反思和团队合作。

感谢何亚男老师、应晓球老师，感谢所有为此付出过努力的老师们，在此我表达由衷的敬意。我也将深入研究，勇于创新，为上海的英语教学添砖加瓦。

汤　青

上海市教育委员会教学研究室英语学科教研员

上海市英语特级教师，正高级教师

2020年6月

丛书前言

随着全国教育改革的不断深化，立德树人的思想渐入人心。中华人民共和国教育部颁布的《普通高中英语课程标准（2017年版2020年修订）》明确指出，高中英语课程的具体目标是培养和发展学生的英语学科核心素养——语言能力、文化意识、思维品质和学习能力。如何顺应时代的呼唤，在英语教学中培育未来世界所需要的人才？如何在我们每天的课堂上将学生学科核心素养的培养落到实处？这些是广大教师都在关心和思考的问题。正是基于这些背景与思考，我们决定出版"落实学科核心素养在课堂"丛书，与广大教师分享我们学习、思考与探究的成果。

"落实学科核心素养在课堂"丛书是在上海市教师专业发展工程领导小组办公室资助、上海教育出版社出版的"高中英语课堂教学设计"丛书的基础上改写、修订、精简而成。"高中英语课堂教学设计"丛书共四册，分别是《高中英语阅读教学设计》《高中英语语法教学活动设计》《高中英语词汇教学活动设计》和《高中英语写作教学设计》。最早出版的《高中英语阅读教学设计》自2010年问世以来已有10年了。但是，每当我们捧起这套沉甸甸的"砖头"丛书，就难忘当年进行这项工作的初衷，努力挑战自我、勤奋学习思考、扎实探索教学、认真撰写修改的一幕幕场景又浮现在眼前。

2006年上海市普教系统"双名工程"启动，在长达十多年的"双名工程"实施过程中，由何亚男、应晓球、张育青、吴彩霞和金怡主持的一至三期英语学科名师培养基地，坚持"名师培育在课堂"的理念，以课题引领为抓手，分别将高中英语教学中的阅读教学、语法教学、词汇教学和写作教学等四个重点问题确立为研究课题，针对教师在教学中的困惑和问题，通过"学习—实践—反思—研究—再实践"，探索和发现解决问题的方法和途径。

我们将研究重点聚焦在"教学设计"上，是因为教学活动是教师实施教学计划、落实课堂教学目标的主要载体，是指导学生学习、掌握和运用英语的主要途径，教学活动设计是教师在日常教学中绕不开的话题。如何进行教学设计，设计什么样的教学活动，如何开展这些教学活动，反映了教师的价值追求、教育思想和理念、教学能力和专业水平，更直接关系到课堂教学的效率和学生学习英语的成效。因此，我们努力通过研究"教学设计"，转变和提升教师的教学理念，增强他们发现和解决问题的意识和能力，提高教学设计和教学实施的能力和水平，最终促进教师形成专业发展的自觉，改进英语课堂教学，让学生学得更有效。在研究过程中，我们收集与分析课堂教学中的问题和现象，例如：阅读教学"重测试轻理解"、语法教学"重规则轻语用"、词汇教学"重讲解轻使用"、写作教学"重结果轻过程"等问题普遍存在，严重影响了学生的英语学习。关于教学设计，教师也存在许多认识的误区和困惑，比如：设计教学活动的原则和依据是什么？如何评价教学活动的有效性？如何根据不同课型、不同内容及不同要求，设计符合学生需求的教学活动？

为了解决这些问题，名师培养基地组织学员学习英语教学前沿理论，根据研究课题重点精读了以下理论原著：*Explore Second Language Reading: Issues and Strategies*，*Text Features and Reading Comprehension*，*Planning Lessons for a Reading Class*，*Learning Vocabulary in Another Language*，*Managing Vocabulary Learning*，*Teaching Language From Grammar to Grammaring*，*Intervening to Help in the Writing Process*。这些书有一个共同特点：既有理论阐述，又很"接地气"、有很强的实践性。它们所传递的文本分析、活动设计及ACTIVE阅读策略，三维语法教学观，通过听、说、读、写多渠道进行词汇教学的策略，过程写作教学法等理念及教学策略，与英语教学深化改革的目标要求高度契合，具有很强的指导意义。教学理论的学习大大提升了我们对于阅读教学、语法教学、词汇教学和写作教学的认识，促使我们重新审视课堂教学和活动设计；教学实践的探索则帮助名师培养基地在提升课堂品质及英语教和学效果的过程中推进了英语教学研究，影响和带动了一大批教师的专业发展。经过上述理论学习与实践探索，融合一线优秀骨干教师的智慧和心血，我们最终形成研究成果——"高中英语课堂教学设计"丛书。十年来，这套书已成为许多英语教师答疑解惑的读本，以及进行教学设计时参考、借鉴的案头书，受到了广泛的认可和推崇。这些教学探究，为我们今天学习与落实新课标奠定了基础，提供了经验和案例。从落实新课标的视角来审视这套丛书，它依然具有不可忽略的参考和借鉴价值。

随着教学改革和研究的不断推进和深化，教师对教学的认识与理解也在逐步发生变化，我们的课堂也在悄然发生变化。以高中英语阅读教学为例，曾几何时，教师拿到阅读文本备课时所做的第一件事就是划下语篇中的语言点，把语言输入作为阅读教学唯一重要的教学目标；后来教师意识到，阅读不仅是语言输入的主要渠道，还是培养学生阅读策略和能力的主要途径；随后，如何在阅读教学中提升学生的情感、态度与价值观，成为教师重视的问题；近年来，语篇文化内涵的理解、深度阅读、学生思维品质的培养成为了阅读教学的关注点。这些变化都说明，形势在发展，教育在变革，对于教师教学能力和专业素养的要求也随之提高。我们还面临许多问题，必须与时俱进，不断进取。

面临新形势的挑战，我们在思考：如何充分利用现有的优质资源，使其在助推英语教学深化改革方面发挥作用，使广大教师在"仰望星空"的同时"脚踏实地"地在课堂大有作为，将学生英语学科核心素养的培养落到实处；我们在行动：在已有的研究成果"高中英语课堂教学设计"丛书的基础上，组织撰写、分期出版"落实学科核心素养在课堂"丛书。这套丛书的书名有两个关键词——"学科核心素养"和"课堂"，这两个关键词清晰地凸显了本套丛书的编写意图及特点。

首先，这套丛书将聚焦"学科核心素养的培养"，基于高中英语教学的发展和变化，以及对于新课标的学习和领悟，诠释高中英语阅读教学、语法教学、词汇教学、听说教学和写作教学与学科核心素养培养的关系，说明在上述教学中落实学科核心素养培养的途径、方法和策略。其次，本套丛书将延续"高中英语课堂教学设计"丛书的特点，聚焦"课堂"和"教学设计"，针对教师在当下课堂中遇到的困惑和问题，凸显"学科核心素养培养"与"课堂"的关系，在新课标的理念、目标要求及实施意见与我们的日常课堂教学之间搭建桥梁。通过大量的教学实践案例，帮助教师更具体地领悟到课堂是落实学科核心素养培养的主要渠道，分享在课堂中培养学生必备品格与关键能力的有效策略和方法。再次，我们充分考虑了一线教师的实际需求和原丛书的特点，对原丛书四册采取不同的改编和撰写方法。例如，对于《落实学科核心素养在课堂·高中英语阅读教学》《落实学科核心素养在课堂·高中英语语法教学》和《落实学科核心素养在课堂·高中英语词汇教学》这三本书，我们重新组织构建了全书的写作体例和内容框架；而对于《落实学科核心素养在课堂·高中英语写作教学》一书，则采取了重写"综述篇"、精简"实践篇"的方法。另外，本套丛书新增听说教学分册《落实学科核心素养在课堂·高中英语听说教学》，由上海市普教系统第四期"双名工程"英语名师培养基地金怡老师主持的攻关项目组负责撰写。同时，为了让本套丛书更方便教师查阅和携带，我们采取了"瘦身"的措施，浓缩了内容使书变薄、变轻。因此，"落实学科核心素养在课堂"丛书可以称作"高中英语课堂教学设计"丛书的升级版。最后，为了更好地体现继承与发展的关系，本套丛书主编由原丛书的主编何亚男和应晓球担任，编写组成员由原上海市"双名工程"名师培养基地主持人、学员，以及参与过编写工作的老师组成，他们是张育青、吴彩霞、金怡、陆跃勤、孟莎、沈冬梅、金敏、张珏恩、黄岳辉、楼蕾、吴喆、郝民、钱海珍等。这些老师了解本套丛书的"前世今生"，也是当前英语教学改革的积极参与者和引领者，他们的加盟必定会使这套丛书更接地气，更具针对性。我们还特聘了德高望重的英语特级教师吴小英老师作为顾问，她的真知灼见给了我们很多启示。

我们真心希望这套丛书能为一线教师答疑解惑，激发和促进广大教师对于在英语课堂中落实学科核心素养培养问题的深层次思考和探究！让我们共同努力，打造有利于学生健康成长的充满活力和智慧的课堂！

最后，衷心感谢上海市普教系统一至三期"双名工程"英语名师培养基地的学员，以及在过去十多年中与我们一起奋斗、努力的老师们！感恩有你们的参与、信任和陪伴。衷心感谢曾给予我们无私帮助和悉心指导的英语教学领域的专家学者们！感恩有你们的理解、指引和帮助。衷心感谢汤青老师为我们作序！感恩你长期以来的支持和帮助。最后，衷心感谢上海教育出版社十多年来对我们的支持！

"落实学科核心素养在课堂"丛书编委会

2020 年 8 月

前　言

　　英语写作能力是指在社会情境中用英语书面表达意义、意图、情感和态度的能力。提升学生的英语写作能力是英语教学中培养学生听、说、读、看和写等语言技能的重要任务之一，也是贯彻实施高中英语新课标、培养学生必备品格和关键能力、落实学科核心素养的一个重要载体。"写"作为英语语言能力中的一项输出性技能，在缺乏语言运用的学习环境中更难获得。长期以来，高中英语写作教学现状不尽如人意，主要表现为教学理念陈旧、教学方法单一、教学效率低下等，成为高中英语教学的重点和难点问题。

　　2012年，第三期"上海市普教系统名校长名师培养工程"启动。由何亚男、金怡、张育青、吴彩霞所主持的中学英语一组和二组基地秉承"以问题为导向、以任务为驱动"的培训策略，把高中英语写作教学研究纳入五年培养计划，以探索提炼高中英语写作教学的有效策略与方法为主要研究内容，以出版《高中英语写作教学设计》一书为主要的预期研究成果。基地主持人带领学员，通过"学习—实践—反思—研究—再实践"的培训模式，围绕高中英语写作教学开展了有序的研究探索活动。一是认真读书学习。我们学习了有关英语写作教学前沿理论与方法的专著，包括Arthur Brookes和Peter Crundy合著的《英语写作教学》、Antonia Chandrasegaran所著的《写作过程中的教师介入》、Jeremy Harmer所著的《如何教写作》，以及Write Source等。之后开展读书心得交流会、专家写作教学专题讲座等活动，提升学员对英语写作教学理论与方法的认识和理解；二是扎实地进行写作教学实践研究。我们将理论与实践相结合，不仅基地学员在自己的课堂上多次实践，还联合学员所在学校、所在区的一线教师和区名师工作室共同参与研究，内化理论和方法；三是深入开展实践后反思。根据学员和一线教师们的实践体验和研讨，基地组织大型写作教学专题论坛，总结经验，反思不足，领悟提高；四是及时研究提炼形成策略和方法。通过总结和反思，学员和一线教师们及时撰写写作教学体会、案例和论文，或完成子课题研究,实现从感性到理性的转变;五是再实践再提升。为了完善写作教学研究,推广研究成果,基地与上海市复兴高级中学、上海市宜川中学等多所学校联合举办了"高中英语写作教学实践研究"专题活动,与河南、内蒙、宁夏等地进行跨省市的教学实践和研讨,还联合杭州外国语学校进行"关注过程、激活思维、合理介入——浙沪高中英语写作课堂教学实践"研究,并将研究成果通过讲座和工作坊的方式对辽宁、贵州等省市进行教研辐射。经过三年多的执着探索与研究,在英语学科专家陈洁倩、吴小英、魏孟勋、宋凤、徐欣幸等老师们的悉心指导和帮助下,学员对写作教学形成了新的认识和理解,并在教学实践中运用、总结、提炼,又通过跨校、跨区、跨省市的思维火花碰撞和智慧共享,经过反复磨稿、讨论和修改,最终在2017年将研究成果《高中英语写作教学设计》一书献给广大英语教师。

《落实学科核心素养在课堂·高中英语写作教学》是"落实学科核心素养在课堂"丛书之一,旨在帮助英语教师领悟他们在现代教育背景下的使命和责任、写作教学的目标和要求、理念与方法,探索、研究和分享如何在课堂中落实学科核心素养的培养,以及有效开展写作教学的途径与方法。本书编写组针对广大一线教师在写作教学中的问题和困惑,依据中华人民共和国教育部颁布的《普通高中英语课程标准(2017年版2020年修订)》(下面简称"高中英语新课标")对于英语写作教学提出的目标要求,对《高中英语写作教学设计》一书进行了修改和精简,体现了与时俱进的追求和特点,并且更方便教师使用。本书分为两大部分——"综述篇"和"实践篇",与原书相比,本书主要有以下变化:1)重构综述篇。本部分由上海市奉贤中学吴彩霞撰写,作者基于高中英语新课标的要求重新撰写了综述篇,简明地阐述了英语学科核心素养培养与写作教学的关系,并针对当前写作教学中存在的问题和弊病,探讨了在写作教学中落实学科核心素养培养的主要方法、途径与策略;2)精简实践篇。本部分由上海市奉贤中学张育青统稿,保留原书各种文体的写作要点、写作技巧及部分精选的训练范例;精简了描述、记叙、说明、议论、应用等五类文体写作的教学实践案例。

《落实学科核心素养在课堂·高中英语写作教学》一书具有以下特点:1)教育理念先进。帮助教师进一步认识到写作教学是培养学生语言能力、文化意识、思维品质和学习能力的载体,并明确其实施的方法和途径,有助于将学科核心素养培养真正落实在写作教学的课堂上;2)理论联系实际。以过程写作教学法为指导，注重写作教学过程中的活动设计和教师的适时介入，注重学生自我反思、自我修正等学习能力的培养和提升；3）契合教学需要。依据高中英语新课标要求，从高中英语写作中描述、记叙、说明、议论、应用等五种常见写作类型入手，介绍不同文体的写作要点和写作技巧，每个写作技巧都配有练习活动和参考答案，最后呈现完整的写作教学实践案例，加深教师对过程写作设计和教学操作要领的理解。全书理念与时俱进，理论结合实践；既有具体的教学技巧讲解与训练，又有完整的教学设计和实施案例，可供一线英语教师教学参考或直接应用于教学中。

简而言之，《落实学科核心素养在课堂·高中英语写作教学》凝聚了第三期"双名工程"英语学科名师培养基地学员和专家导师们的智慧和心血，也体现了本书编写组在英语教学深化改革背景下新的思考和追求。我们真诚地希望《落实学科核心素养在课堂·高中英语写作教学》一书能成为广大英语教师的益友，并通过本书的读者传播高中英语新课标背景下的教学理念、方法和策略以及实践探索成果，为培养学生面向未来的必备品格和关键能力而共同努力！

《落实学科核心素养在课堂·高中英语写作教学》编写组

2020年5月

目　录

第一章 综　　述

一、英语学科核心素养培养与写作教学

（一）英语学科核心素养和写作能力

国家教育部正式颁布的《普通高中英语课程标准（2017年版2020年修订）》（以下简称"高中英语新课标"）指出："学科核心素养是学科育人价值的集中体现，是学生通过学科学习而逐步形成的正确价值观念、必备品格和关键能力。英语学科核心素养主要包括语言能力、文化意识、思维品质和学习能力。"其中，语言能力指"在社会情境中，以听、说、读、看、写等方式理解和表达意义的能力，以及在学习和使用语言的过程中形成的语言意识和语感"。五种语言技能中，听、读、看是理解性技能，说和写是表达性技能。作为英语学科核心素养的基础要素之一，也作为一项重要的表达性技能，"写"承载着"表情达意"的重要任务，学生无论走上社会还是走向世界，无论在生活中还是在工作中，都会有情感交流、思想交流和文化交流的需要，写作就是他们必备的重要能力之一。写作能力的提高蕴含着文化意识、思维品质和学习能力的提升，有助于学生成为更好的思想者、学习者和跨文化交际者。因此，从学生的终身发展来看，无论将来从事什么职业，他们都应该掌握写作技能，切实提高运用英语的能力，为真实的语言交际打好基础。

高中英语新课标对于表达性技能提出了明确的内容要求，其中与"写"有关的表述如下表所示：

课程类别	语言技能内容要求
必修	<ul><li>清楚地描述事件的过程；</li><li>使用文字和非文字手段描述个人经历和事物特征；</li><li>在书面表达中借助连接性词语、指示代词、词汇衔接等语言手段建立逻辑关系；</li><li>在书面表达中借助标题、图标、图像、表格、版式等传递信息、表达意义；</li><li>根据表达目的选择适当的语篇类型；</li><li>根据表达的需要选择词汇和语法结构；</li><li>根据表达的需要选择正式语或非正式语。</li></ul>

（续表）

课程类别	语言技能内容要求
选择性必修	• 以书面形式描述、概括经历和事实； • 以书面形式传递信息、论证观点、表达情感； • 通过重复、举例和解释等方式澄清意思； • 运用语篇衔接手段，提高表达的连贯性； • 根据表达意图和受众特点，有意识地选择和运用语言； • 根据表达的需要，设计合理的语篇结构； • 在书面表达中有目的地利用标题、图标、图表、版式、字体和字号等手段有效地传递信息、表达意义。
选修（提高类）	• 通过书面方式再现想象的经历和事物； • 以书面形式对观点、事件、经历进行评论； • 通过罗列、举例、对比等方式进行论证； • 借助词语和句式形象地传递自己的情感和思想； • 根据需要创建出不同形式的语篇； • 根据需要使用委婉语、模糊语； • 使用衔接手段有效提高语篇的连贯性； • 使用特殊词汇、语法进行创造性地表达； • 使用图像、图表等非文字资源创造性地表达意义。

高中英语新课标对于高中英语学业质量水平提出了具体要求，其中与"写"有关的描述如下表所示：

学业质量水平	质量描述
水平一	• 能以书面形式简要描述自己或他人的经历，表达观点并举例说明；能介绍中外主要节日和中华优秀传统文化；书面表达中所用词汇和语法结构能够表达主要意思； • 能运用语篇的衔接手段构建书面语篇、表达意义，体现意义的逻辑关联性；能借助多模态语篇资源提高表达效果。
水平二	• 能在书面表达中有条理地描述自己或他人的经历，阐述观点，表达情感态度；能描述事件发生、发展的过程；能描述人或事物的特征、说明概念；能概述所读语篇的主要内容或续写语篇； • 能在表达过程中有目的地选择词汇和语法结构，确切表达意思，体现意义的逻辑关联性；能使用多模态语篇资源，达到特殊的表达效果。
水平三	• 能通过书面方式再现想象的经历和事物，对事实、观点、经历进行评论；能根据需要创建不同形式的语篇； • 能使用衔接手段有效提高书面语篇的连贯性；能使用特殊词汇、语法创造性地表达意义。

从以上高中英语新课标对学生英语写作能力的具体要求中可以看出，写作教学是高中英语教学非常重要的一个组成部分。作为高中英语教师，必须在深入学习高中英语新课标关于学科核心素养培养要求的基础上，了解英语写作教学的规律并探索英语写作教学的有效途径和方法。

（二）指向英语学科核心素养培养的写作教学

既然学生在英语写作中要运用语言来表情达意，那么我们一方面可以将写作教学视为培育学科核心素养的中介与手段，借助一系列写作教学活动来培养学生的学科核心素养，达成教育的根本目标；另一方面，将培养"写作能力""写作素养"作为写作教学目标，基于学情，探索并实践有效的途径和方法，培养学生的写作素养和能力。

1. 写作教学中语言能力的培养

写作，作为一种书面表达方式，具有多种文体，包括记叙文、议论文、说明文等；作为一种交流手段，又具有多种功能，按其功能可分为功能性写作（如新闻报道、报告、论文）、私人写作（如家人、朋友之间的书信）、公共写作（如通知、海报）等类型。

在写作过程中，学生不仅需要运用所学的语言知识（词汇、语法、语篇和语用知识等）传递信息，表达个人观点、意图和态度以及抒发情感，还需要根据不同的写作对象、写作文体功能以及写作要求，选择、运用恰当的语言与读者进行有效的交流与沟通。毋庸置疑，写作教学在培养和提升学生语言意识与语感、提高语言能力方面有着不可或缺的地位和作用。

2. 写作教学中文化意识的培养

根据高中英语新课标，文化意识指"对中外文化的理解和对优秀文化的认同，是学生在全球化背景下表现出的跨文化认知、态度和行为取向"。培养文化意识的目标是使学生获得文化知识，理解文化内涵，形成正确的价值观，具备一定的跨文化沟通和传播中华文化的能力。

在写作过程中，学生需要意识到来自不同国家、民族的读者具有不同的文化、习俗和观念，并根据不同的场合、背景运用恰当的语言，得体地传递信息、表达思想和情感，进行跨文化交流。因此，写作教学是培养和增强学生文化意识、提升文化素养的重要渠道，也是提高学生综合语言运用能力，为将来跨文化交流打下扎实基础的重要一环。

3. 写作教学中思维品质的培养

高中英语新课标对思维品质的定义是"思维在逻辑性、批判性、创新性等方面所表现出来的能力和水平"。思维品质的发展有助于提升学生分析和解决问题的能力，使他们能够从跨文化视角观察和认识世界，对事物作出正确的价值判断。培养思维品质，即要求学生能够梳理、概括信息，建构新概念，分析、推断信息之间的逻辑关系，正确评判各种思想观点，创造性地表达自己的观点，具备多元思维的意识和创新思维的能力。

在写作过程中，学生需要开动脑筋去思考和分析问题、梳理和归纳信息、审视和评判观点等。学生不仅需要思考写作目的、读者期待、主题思想，构思写作内容、篇章结构，还需要不断地选择、提炼、修改语言等，使表达更清晰、有条理、合逻辑。因此，写作的全过程无不涉及思维活动和思维品质的培养。

4. 写作教学中学习能力的培养

根据高中英语新课标，学习能力指学生"积极运用和主动调适英语学习策略、拓宽英语学习渠道、努力提升英语学习效率的意识和能力"。高中英语新课标对学习能力提出了明确的目标，要求学生能够"选择恰当的策略与方法，监控、评价、反思和调整自己的学习内容和进程"。

美国第二语言写作评价专家Sara Cushing Weigle（2002）曾指出，语言交际能力是语言知识和策略能力相互作用的结果。在写作过程中，学生除了要运用适当的认知策略，还需运用一定的元认知策略来评价、反思和调控写作内容和进程，如写前计划构思、列出写作提纲，写中发现具体问题、探究原因和调整方案、运用写作策略和技巧，写后自我检查、同伴互评、修改等。因此，写作教学是培养学生良好的写作习惯和自主学习能力的重要抓手。

二、基于英语学科核心素养培养的写作教学

为了有效提升学生的写作能力，培养学生的英语学科核心素养，教师必须树立"写作是一个过程"的理念并将其转化为实际的教学行为。在写作教学过程中，教师要加强介入，及时发现学生写作过程中存在的问题和困难，并给予适时的帮助和指导。同时，教师要注意培养学生写作时的读者意识，注重写作教学活动的设计，开展以学生为主体的过程性评价。

（一）开展过程性写作教学

长期以来，尽管英语写作教学受到了教师的关注，但是"重结果、轻过程"

的现象依然普遍存在，教师对写作教学的思考和研究不足。纵观现状，写作教学中主要存在以下三个问题：

一是缺乏针对性的写作技能教学。日常教学中，教师很少开设专门的写作课，即使偶尔进行写作指导也往往是笼统地讲授一些写作的"套路"和"套句"，缺乏有针对性的、具体的写作技能教学。不同的文体有不同的写作要求，需要运用不同的写作技能。例如，在描述性写作中，学生需学会运用视觉、听觉、嗅觉、触觉等感官细节（sensory details）生动、形象、直观地描写人物、事物和场景等；在记叙文写作中，学生不仅需知晓记叙文的"六要素"（when, where, who, what, why, how），还需学会运用对话、设置悬念、制造冲突等方法，围绕主题生动叙述并挖掘其深刻含义，或借物抒情，或托物言志；在议论文写作中，教师不能只是简单、机械地介绍议论文"三段式"结构，而忽略相关技能的教学，例如：如何用简明的语言写好含有中心论点的主题句（thesis statement），如何用不同的方法说明和支撑论点等。以上这些写作技能的教学都需要教师根据学生实际在课堂中加以规划和落实。

二是缺乏对写作的过程性指导。写作是一个过程，从计划构思、拟写草稿，到修改文稿、编辑校订等阶段，学生会遇到内容组织或语言表达上的各种问题，每一个阶段都需要教师的引领和指导，例如：指导学生列出具有逻辑性的写作提纲，引导他们在写出初稿后进行自我修正和改进等。然而，目前写作教学往往是简单的"三部曲"：教师简单布置写作任务—学生直接开始写作—教师批改学生作文，或进行简短的头脑风暴（brainstorming）活动后立刻让学生开始写作，而鲜有指导他们如何进行文章整体构思、确定主要内容、理清逻辑关系，进而列出显示文章内容提要和整体框架的写作提纲。

三是缺乏有效的评价方式。有效的评价可以促进学生写作并对写作教学产生反拨作用。目前，教师批改评分是主要甚至唯一的评价手段。教师费时费力地改了一叠又一叠的作文，学生往往只是看一眼分数或不甚理解的评语后便束之高阁。这样的评价方式对于学生写作水平的提高收效甚微。在写作教学中，教师应该开展以学生为主体的过程性评价，组织、指导学生通过自评或互评发现问题并进行改进，逐步提升写作能力。

总之，学生写作能力不甚理想的一个主要原因就是教师"重结果、轻过程"，忽视对写作过程的分析、研究和设计所造成的。

以交互理论（Interaction Theory）为基础的"过程写作教学法"认为，写作的过程实质上是群体间的交际活动，而不是写作者的单独行为（何亚男 等，2017）。这种交互式写作教学的主要目的是让学生能够在过程中体验、发现和创造，并把自己的思想情感传递给他人，以实现用书面语言进行人际交往的目的。过程写作教学法把写作看作是一种复杂的、循环往复的且富有创造性的行为，是写作者不断地作出选择、修改、决定并反复循环的过程，是写作者运用策略管理写作的过程，是写作者探索发现、自主监控、自我反思、自觉调适的一系列行为，是一个相当复杂的心理认知过程和语言交际过程，它所注重的是写作者在写作过程中的经历、体验和感悟。

过程性写作教学主张，写作教学要研究学生在写作过程中应该做什么、怎么做，突出学生写作策略培养和教师全程指导的重要性。它更关注的是过程（process）而不是最终的成品（product）。它强调好的作品总要经历反复构思、修改等过程，而非一蹴而就的。过程性写作教学包含一系列的活动：确立目标（setting goals）、构思内容（generating ideas）、组织信息（organizing information）、选择语言（selecting appropriate language）、拟写草稿（making a draft）、阅读检查（reading and reviewing）和修改编辑（revising and editing）。

关于过程性写作的步骤，不同的研究者有不同的划分，但是大致都包含了以下四个循环往复、交互渗透的阶段：

1. 计划构思（Planning）

1）明确写作目的与阅读对象

教师要引导学生明确写作目的，这能帮助学生选择正确的文体，紧扣主题选择相关的内容和表达方式等。同时，要引导学生考虑写作的读者对象，针对来自不同的教育、文化、社会背景的读者，选用恰当的语言和语气，以便得体、有效地与之交流。

2）收集、分类、组织写作素材

教师要引导学生根据写作目的和阅读对象，通过讨论（discussing）、列清单（listing）、画思维导图（mind mapping）等方式开展头脑风暴，开阔思路。围绕写作主题，收集、分类、组织相关事实、细节等信息作为论据和素材，为后续写作做好准备。

3）构思文章结构与主旨内容

在前面两步的基础上，教师需引导学生着手构思文章结构与主旨内容。编写清晰又合理的提纲有助于学生从整体上构建文章框架和脉络，避免写作内容的遗漏、重复或前后矛盾。一篇好的提纲能够较为完整、全面、清楚地规划和编排文章结构和主旨内容，体现文章各部分的逻辑关系，使写作者能够据此进行材料的筛选。

2. 拟写草稿（Drafting）

明确了写作目的、读者、文体、文章主旨与结构之后，便可开始拟写草稿。此时，写作者必须围绕主题展开分析、说明、描写或论述。教师在这一阶段要引导学生带着读者意识，并根据所确定的主旨和提纲组织细节进行写作，关注的重点应放在思路的清晰、内容的恰当和行文的流畅上，而不应过多关注语法纠错。

3. 修改文稿（Revising）

在此阶段，写作者对初稿进行修改完善。学生应认真阅读全文，审视文章主题是否鲜明、内容是否充实切题、结构是否合理、逻辑条理是否清晰。同时，要关注语言表达的正确性、多样性和流畅性。例如，句子结构是否正确、多样，用词是否恰当等。教师可以使用检查列表等评价工具指导学生进行自我检查和修正或同伴互评，优化所写的文章。

4. 编辑校订（Editing）

在这一阶段，写作者通过校对阅读（proofread）对文章进行编辑校对、修改润色并最后定稿。教师要引导学生检查单词拼写、大小写、标点符号、前后一致性、用词、句子结构、语法（如语态、时态、单复数）等方面是否有错误或不恰当的地方，并加以修改。

需要特别强调的是，写作过程的四个阶段应该按照学生的英语学习基础和写作教学的具体目标逐步开展和推进，而不是一堂课所能完全体现或短时间内所能完成的，开展过程性写作教学是一个长期的过程。同时，在写作过程中，四个阶段不一定呈线性排列，而往往是循环往复的。换言之，学生从计划构思、拟写草稿、修改文稿到编辑校订，往往是反复轮回进行，是一个不断思考、修改、调整的过程。

（二）加强写作过程中的教师介入

根据认知心理学的观点，写作就是写作者做出一个又一个决定（a series of decisions and choices）的过程（Flower & Hayes, 1981）。无论是写私人信件还是学术论文，写作者都需要决定如何开头、如何组织结构、如何结尾、如何取舍信息、如何遣词造句、如何吸引读者等。同时，还需根据写作目的、文章体裁、读者期待等，学会识别并修改不太恰当的决定。因此，写作是一个复杂的过程，在这一过程中学生必然会面临各种困难和问题。当学生不知如何做出正确决定或已经做出错误决定时，教师需及时介入，给予适时的帮助。

教师介入是指在写作过程的不同阶段（计划构思、拟写草稿、修改文稿、编辑校订），给予学生适时的引导，帮助他们围绕写作目的、主旨思想、内容结构、语言表达等方面，做出正确的决定。

写作过程中教师要实施有效的介入，关键在于选择介入的内容（what）、时间（when）和方式（how）。

1. 介入内容（What）

教师应该选择哪些方面的内容进行介入才比较合理、有效呢？

首先，要根据写作文体的特点确定介入内容。写作有多种文体，如记叙文、议论文、说明文、应用文、描述性文章等。写作文体不同，其写作要求与特点也不同。例如，说明文以解释、说明为主要的表达方式，是对事物科学、客观、清晰的阐释或解说；记叙文是以叙述事件或经历为主要内容，并描述人物思想情感的文体，一般按时间顺序展开；而议论文通常由论点、论据和论证三大要素构成，其特点是以评析、论述的方式表达作者的观点并说服读者。因此，教师要抓住不同文体的特点实施介入。

例如，进行议论文写作时，要抓住议论文的主要特点，如论点、论据等。这时教师介入的内容就是引导学生判断文章是否有明确的论点，以及相关且充分的论据。如果文章没有论点，教师需帮助学生理清思路，提出自己的想法和观点；如果文章有论点但是论据不充分或相关性不大，则可以组织学生与同伴或全班讨论交流，删除无关或相关性不大的内容，增补和论点有密切关联的事实、数据、案例或名言作为论据，并根据论点合理安排次序。

其次，选择高水平信息（high-level message）或整体目标（global goal）进行介入。在写作中，高水平信息或整体目标通常指如何表达、发展中心思想，如何组织或重组文章结构等，以便取得写作总体上的满意效果。相反，单词拼写、介词用法或标点符号是否正确被称为低水平信息（low-level message）或局部目标（local goal）（Chandrasegaran, 2007）。教师介入时主要关注高水平信息或整体目标而不是低水平信息或局部目标。当教师指导学生选择并决定写作内容和语言时，对高水平信息或整体目标的介入更能有效帮助学生提高写作水平。例如，在投诉信这一应用文写作的过程中，教师发现学生的作文有时态错误、主谓不一致、语句不连贯、投诉内容不具体等问题。这时教师应该选择哪些方面介入呢？哪些是高水平信息？显然，投诉缘由、诉求和解决方案是投诉信的写作目的和主要内容。此时，教师不妨让学生暂时停笔并提出下列活动要求，进行介入：

- Describe to your partner the specific problems of the product you have bought or the bad service you have received as well as the time or place that all this happened.
- Tell your partner a possible solution you expect to your complaint in as few words as possible.
- Read your letter. Locate and change words or expressions that are too general, too vague or subjective when you are complaining.

以上三个活动都聚焦在高水平信息上，即投诉内容、解决方案以及应用文的语言特点，引导学生用具体、客观、简要的语言进行写作。

2. 介入时间（When）

关于教师介入的时间，要考虑介入的频率和介入的时间节点。

显而易见，教师应该在每一节写作课中都有所介入。这样，学生在教师的适时帮助下，可以及时发现和解决写作过程中产生的困难和问题。此外，对于一些重要的写作技能，也需要教师不断反复的指导，学生才能真正掌握。

那么，每一堂课的教师介入应该在什么时间节点呢？根据有关研究，适时有效的教师介入通常发生在学生写作的过程中，即当学生写了一部分或处在构思、修改的过程中（Chandrasegaran，2007）。只有这时，教师才能发现学生遇到的真实困难和问题，如主题思想不清楚、不突出，结构不完整、欠合理等。这时，学生迫切希望得到帮助和指导，以便"步入正轨"，以解"燃眉之急"。如果教师在学生完成作文上交后再批改评价，那时"生米已经煮成了熟饭"，肯定收效甚微。例如，在议论文写作时，如发现学生不能开门见山地表达自己的观点，那么教师应在学生刚刚写了一至两段时就介入，因为这个问题若不及时解决就会影响整篇文章的写作。但如果教学的重点在于如何写好结尾段，那么教师介入的时间则要放在学生写完全文之后。因此，教师应该对照写作教学目标、教学重点和写作技能的教学要求，及时发现学生的问题，在他们最需要帮助的时候适时介入。这样，教师的介入便如"及时雨"，效果显著。

3. 介入方式（How）

教师在学生写作过程中的介入，可以通过明确的指令语、教授写作知识和示范展示等方式进行，帮助学生解决问题，改进写作（Chandrasegaran, 2007）。

1）通过明确的指令语，引导学生发现写作中的问题。

当教师在课堂上发现学生写作中的问题时，可以设计教学活动并通过明确、具体、清晰的指令语，引导学生通过活动发现问题并及时修正。请比较下列两栏中的指令语：

Instructions (A)	Instructions (B)
Please center around the topic in your writing.	Please discuss in pairs what your thesis statement exactly means.
Please make your writing persuasive.	Please give at least two facts or examples to support your idea.
Please pay attention to the structure of your writing.	Please be sure that your writing has an introductory paragraph, a body and an ending. If not, please add one.
Please write clearly and logically.	Please tell your partner whether your writing is developed in order of cause and effect. If not, find out the cause and effect and write again in order of cause and effect.
Please make your writing as natural as possible.	Please locate transitional words that connect different ideas or sentences. If you fail to find one or some, please try to use transitional words where necessary.

不难看出，A栏的指令语笼统、含糊，缺乏操作性，而B栏的指令语则具体、指向明确，这样的指令语才能有效地帮助学生对照检查、发现和修正问题，具有直接的指导意义。

2）通过教授写作知识，引导学生做出更好的选择。

为了帮助学生解决写作中的困难和问题，教师需根据写作教学目标和要求有计划地教授必要的写作知识，帮助学生循序渐进地学习和掌握所需的写作技能。例如，不同文体的篇章结构和写作特点、文章的连贯性和一致性、过渡词的使用等语篇知识，以及主题句的撰写、修辞手法的运用和用词等等，都需教师科学规划、逐步推进，通过系统的教授，帮助学生学会写作，提高写作水平。

3）通过示范展示，引导学生积极参与。

教师的示范展示也是一种有效的介入方式。通过示范展示，学生更容易明白教师的意图，理解写作知识从而改进自己的写作。这一介入方式的运用，关键之一是要选好示范展示的样本。样本可以选自学生当堂写作的作文，也可以选自前几届学生的作文。样本应该代表学生的不同基础和水平，或作为学生可以模仿、借鉴的优秀范文，或能够反映学生写作中普遍、突出的问题。同时，在示范、展示的过程中，教师要引导学生积极参与，在思考、讨论、交流的活动过程中理解、体会、领悟教师的指导，舍弃那些含糊不清、似是而非、无关紧要或毫不相干的词、句，甚至段落，在不断肯定和否定的过程中，运用写作技能，发展思维和语言能力。

当然，教师的介入方式不是千篇一律、固定不变的，教师应该根据不同的写作任务、写作阶段、学生基础等，灵活采用合适的介入方式。

（三）强化学生读者意识的培养

读者意识是指写作者在写作时心中要有明确的"读者"概念。这里的"读者"可以是真实的阅读对象，也可以是写作者心中预设的假想对象。教师要培养学生的读者意识，即在写作时心中有读者，关注不同读者（如同学、朋友、老师、前辈、上级领导等）的阅读目的，以及他们期望从阅读中获得什么，并且思考如何采用恰当的语言、语气和写作方式使读者比较容易理解和接受自己的意图及想要表达的思想等。

高中英语新课标在选择性必修课程中对表达性技能的要求中提道："根据表达意图和受众特点，有意识地选择和运用语言。"选择性必修课程对语用知识的要求也提道："能够根据交际对象的身份、事由、正式与非正式程度，选择得体的语言形式进行有效的跨文化交流。"强化写作者读者意识的培养，可以帮助写作者进一步明确写作目的，确定写作内容，选择运用恰当的语言和语气进行得体的表达。

目前，高中英语写作教学中，读者意识的培养比较薄弱，学生往往忽略目标读者，导致所写内容不合适，或所用语言不得体，不能达到书面表达的真正目的。为此，教师要强化学生读者意识的培养。

在写作教学中，为了培养和增强学生的读者意识，可以引导学生思考以下问题：① 读者是谁？有何期待？即明确文章的主旨内容；② 为什么写这篇文章？即明确写作的目的；③ 谁在写这篇文章？即明确写作者的身份地位，以选择适当的语言和语气。在此基础上写出的文章才能更易为读者所理解和接受。试比较以下三个写作任务：

Task 1：你新买的手机出了问题，为此写信给商场经理投诉。

Task 2：写信给某儿童帮困基金会，以中学生的身份申请扶贫基金项目。

Task 3：写信给即将来中国旅游的美国中学生笔友，为他在中国的行程提出建议。

虽然都是写信，但由于目标读者不同，写信的目的和内容也不同（如下表所示）。

写作任务	目标读者和主旨内容	写作目的	写作者身份
Letter 1	商场经理（有关领导） 投诉缘由（手机的质量问题）和要求	希望诉求得以解决	顾客
Letter 2	基金会负责人（上级主管领导） 申请理由和依据	希望得到批准获得扶贫基金	中学生
Letter 3	美国笔友（中学生朋友） 在华旅游建议	希望能给朋友有益的建议和帮助	中学生

很显然，三封信的写作要求完全不同。第一封信的重点是说清楚投诉缘由，即手机的具体质量问题，以及明确直接的解决方案（修理、更换还是赔偿），语言较正式，陈述要客观，语气要委婉；第二封信的目的是获得扶贫基金，因此申请项目的理由，即如何合理利用这笔扶贫基金的计划构想非常重要，语言较正式，要让读者（基金会负责人）感受到你的迫切心情；第三封信是给同龄朋友的建议，内容应聚焦在有吸引力的具体建议上，语言非正式，语气友好真诚。给朋友的信落款用 yours 即可，但另外两封信则需用 respectfully yours 或 sincerely yours 这类的词语，信的格式也会有所差异。由此可见，读者意识能帮助学生准确定位，明确写作目的和内容，增强语用意识，学会用恰当的语言进行人际交流。

（四）注重写作教学活动设计

高中英语新课标指出："活动是英语学习的基本形式，是学习者学习和尝试运用语言理解与表达意义，培养文化意识，发展多元思维，形成学习能力的主要途径。"通过参与活动，学生获得身临其境的体验和感受，更容易掌握语言知识和技能，也能增进同伴之间的交流。

在写作教学的课堂里，活动是学生学习和实践写作技能、运用语言进行得体表达的主要渠道。教师通过所设计的各种活动，帮助和引导学生在提升写作能力的同时，增强语用意识，提升学习能力。*Beginning to Write*一书在讲述"过程性写作"的理念时也多次提到活动设计的重要性。该书作者Arthur Brookes 和 Peter Grundy（1999）认为教师应该把活动设计作为写作课堂的重点，要尽可能地通过活动教授学生写作知识，培养学生写作技能，提高学生写作水平。

在进行课堂教学设计时，教师首先要分析思考写作的主题语境，所写文章的语篇类型和结构，写作时所需的语言知识、相关的文化背景知识、写作技能以及方法策略等，在此基础上确定写作教学的目标和要求，进而设计写作教学活动。活动设计要由浅入深、层层递进，从学习理解类活动过渡到应用实践类活动，循序渐进地提升学生的英语写作能力。

在设计写作教学活动时，各个阶段开展的活动应服务于其教学目标，即所设计的活动应有明确的目标指向。教学目标不同，教学侧重点则不同，活动形式也不同。

1. 计划构思阶段（Planning）：这一阶段的主要目标是激活学生的写作思路，帮助他们明确写作主旨内容，并围绕写作话题，收集写作素材，进行布局构思。为达到这一目标，可设计以下活动：

1）讨论（Discussing）：教师可通过问题讨论激发学生对于写作任务、写作目的和内容的思考，发掘各种可能有用的信息作为写作的素材。

以话题"My opinion on studying abroad"为例，教师提出以下问题组织学生开展小组讨论：

What can you benefit from studying abroad?

What problems or difficulties will you probably meet if you choose to study abroad?

通过讨论，学生可以相互启发、拓展思路，了解出国留学的益处（如学习外语、开阔眼界、增长见识等）和可能面临的问题与困难（如学费、饮食、住宿、安全等），并从中选择写作素材。

2）列清单（Listing）：引导学生就主题进行构思，用短语或短句列出观点或想要描述的人和事等。

以话题"The causes of the increasing number of mobile phone users"为例，学生通过讨论列出以下清单：

- easy to contact
- take a selfie

- convenient
- play games
- watch films
- listen to music
- read books
- WeChat
- read blogs
- pay online
- low price
- affordable
- fashionable
- search for information
- look up new words
- set an alarm clock
- take photos
- recording
- calculating function
- use it as a calendar
- manage money online
- lighting
- easy to carry
- improve work efficiency
- communicate with people
- easy to charge
- user-friendly
- globalization
- learn online
- development of national economy
- rise of people's living standard
- development of high technology

以上清单是学生即时想到的内容，比较繁杂、凌乱，也有重复。教师须引导学生就所列内容进行分类整合和筛选，并按一定顺序（如重要程度、时间顺序、范围大小等）排列。以下是一位学生经老师引导后修改的清单内容：

* convenient:
  - easy to contact
  - easy to carry
  - easy to charge

* multifunctional:
  - search for information
  - look up new words
  - pay online
  - learn online

* affordable:
  - low price
  - rise of people's living standard

以上清单清晰地将手机用户增长的原因分为三大类，即convenient、multifunctional和affordable，并选取了与之最相关的内容。这样条理清晰、内容相关的清单有助于学生接下来撰写结构清晰、内容合理的初稿。

3）思维导图（Mind-mapping）：以形象的思维导图刺激学生快速联想，收集与主题相关的写作素材。

以介绍中国传统节日中秋节（the Mid-Autumn Festival）为例，在教师"如何介绍中秋节"的问题引导下，学生围绕主题画出了以下思维导图：

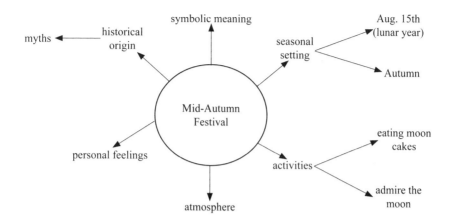

4）自由写作（Free writing）：教师可以让学生围绕写作话题，把所能想到的内容快速地写下来，且不必过分关注逻辑、措辞、语法、拼写等方面，以此激活学生思路，发掘可用素材。

以"作为交换生，你选择去美国还是英国学习"这一话题为例，以下是一位学生自由写作的产出：

If I am given the choice, I prefer to go to Britain for my further study. There are many world-famous universities in England, like Cambridge and Oxford. I can also visit many places of historic interest, such as London Bridge, Buckingham palace, the British museum, Hyidepark and so on. But America is also a good choice. Top universities like Harvard, mashengligong also attracts me a lot. Besides, I dream of having a look at Miss liberty, of course including the white house. In addition, the weather in England in winter is cold and wet, and changeable. Is it still a fog city? Maybe, in America it's more comfortable. To tell the truth, Britain has a long history and a lot of historical buildings, like churches appeal to me so much. And America does not give me a sense of safety because of the terrorism.

不难发现，该生在写作时思维跳跃、缺乏逻辑性，想到哪里写到哪里，一会儿写英国、美国的名牌大学和历史名胜，一会儿写英国的气候、历史和建筑，一会儿又写美国的安全问题，语句组织也不太有条理，还有一些语法、拼写等错误。然而，这些都不是问题，关键是让学生尽量把想到的内容都写下来，然后在老师的指导下，思考并选择与写作主题关系密切的、合适的内容，再加工形成主题突出、合乎逻辑、有说服力的文章。

5）编写提纲（Outlining）：引导学生以提纲形式拟定文章的主要内容、整体结构和材料次序。通过编写提纲，学生能够整理思路，布局篇章结构，确定主要内容。下面是两种常用的提纲形式：

（1）标题式提纲

标题式提纲是用短语作为标题列出文章各部分的内容要点，其特点是文字简洁、耗时不多。编写标题式提纲要求标明段落层次，同一层次至少包括两个并列项。例如：

> **Topic**：The popularity of playing table tennis
>
> Ⅰ. Introduction
>
>   A sport with many advantages
>
> Ⅱ. Development—the advantages of the sport
>
>   A. Benefits to health (lose weight, raise immunity to disease, help one's mind work quickly)
>
>   B. Character building (perseverance, cooperation)
>
>   C. Other advantages (little space occupation and good for all ages)
>
> Ⅲ. Conclusion
>
>   A popular sport good for us all

（2）句子式提纲

所谓句子式提纲就是用完整的句子列出文章各部分的主要内容。这种提纲呈现的内容较具体、明确，各部分之间的关系也较清晰。仍以上一个话题为例：

> **Topic:** The popularity of playing table tennis
>
> Ⅰ. Introduction
>
> Playing table tennis is quite popular in China because it is a sport with many advantages.
>
> Ⅱ. Development
>
>   A. Playing table tennis is of great benefit to one's physical and

mental health.

    1. It helps one lose weight and raise immunity to disease.

    2. It helps one's mind work quickly.

B. Playing table tennis is of great value to building one's character.

    1. It helps one persevere when he meets with difficulties.

    2. It helps one cooperate with each other.

C. There are other advantages of playing table tennis.

    1. It only needs a space of 8 meters in width and 16 meters in length.

    2. It is good for people of all ages, whether young or old.

Ⅲ. Conclusion

That is why so many people take up table tennis in their spare time.

编写提纲是学生思考安排篇章结构的过程。教师需通过适时的介入帮助学生学会围绕文章中心选择材料，思考提纲各个部分之间的逻辑关系，进而修改完善提纲。

2. 拟写草稿阶段（Drafting）：这一阶段的目标是指导学生在计划构思的基础上写出结构完整的初稿。

学生各自独立写作是此阶段的主要教学活动。学生根据所列提纲的结构布局以及所选素材，紧扣主题，将内容细节组句成文，并运用过渡词语（transitional words and phrases）使文章连贯。教师可要求学生隔行撰写，以便添加、改动相关内容。在这一活动中，教师要特别注意以下几点：

* 给学生充足的时间安静写作，不要随意打断他们的思路。

* 注意观察写作进程，在必要时介入，确保学生按所列提纲进行写作。

* 如学生语言表达有困难，可给予个别帮助。

3. 修改文稿阶段（Revising）：这一阶段的目标是指导学生根据要求对写好的初稿进行改进完善。在此阶段，学生重读初稿，重点审视文章的主旨内容和组织结构，同时注意选词的正确性和句子的流畅性，对初稿进行修改。教师则要引导学生通过自评、互评等途径，利用检查列表来发现初稿中的问题并加以修正。

1）制定检查列表（Checklist）

检查列表是帮助学生检查对照和发现写作中的问题的一种常用工具。教师根据本次写作的文体、主题内容及具体要求，与学生共同讨论和确定修改初稿的标准，并将主要关注点一一列出，制定出一份检查列表。教师可以采用不同的方法开展这项活动。例如：通过复习回顾在计划构思和拟写草稿阶段的学习活动，再次明确写作要求；以优秀范文为例，凸显标准和要求；选择具有典型问题的学生初稿为例，使制定的检查列表更贴近实际，更易于学生理解、接受和使用。检查列表的制定过程，是教师引导学生再次明确写作要求的过程。因此，无论教师用哪一种方法，学生的参与都尤为重要，学生参与制定的检查列表对于修改作文的指导作用也是最大的。

检查列表的内容除了应涵盖主题是否鲜明、组织结构是否合理且符合逻辑、内容是否充实、用词是否恰当等方面，还要突出本次写作的特定要求以及学生写作中存在的问题，比如：（描述性文章）是否恰当使用了感官词？（投诉信）表述是否客观？（议论文）论点是否清晰、论据是否充分？等等。这样的检查列表才能对学生修改作文有所帮助。

2）利用检查列表进行修改

修改初稿是写作教学过程中不可或缺的重要环节。学生通过仔细重读初稿，审视自己在写初稿时心中是否有读者、所写内容是否与原定目标一致、是否突出了主题、是否达到了预设读者的期望，以及如果没有，问题在哪里，然后进行自我修正。这样的修改活动不仅有助于学生加强读者意识、提升写作能力和水平，还能促进学生形成自我慎思的思辨能力。

在这一活动中，教师要引导学生根据所制定的检查列表，进行对照检查和修改。学生自我修改、同伴互改、教师指导修改，这些都是常用的方式。同时，教师要根据课堂情况及时组织多渠道的交流反馈，如在学生自我修改的基础上进行小组研读、交流与评价，选择学生的修改稿展开班级讨论等。总之，始终以学生为主体，促进学生对自己的作品进行反思与自我修正，提高写作能力。

4. 编辑校订阶段（Editing）：编辑校订阶段是学生对所写文章进行最后检查、修改、润色及定稿的阶段。学生通过校阅（proofread）文章的修改稿，仔细检查并改正语法结构、单词拼写、标点符号、大小写等方面存在的错误，最后誊清定稿。教师可利用检查列表或同伴互阅等方式，指导学生完成这一学习任务。

与修改文稿阶段不同，这一阶段所使用的检查列表更多地关注语法结构、单词拼写、标点符号、大小写等方面的内容，列表可以包括下列问题：

1. Do all my sentences end with end punctuation?

2. Do I use commas after introductory word groups or transitions?

3. Do all my sentences begin with capital letters?

4. Do I spell all the words correctly?

5. Do I use correct forms of verbs?

6. Do the subjects and verbs of all the sentences agree in number?

...

在这一阶段，教师还可引导学生在定稿前，对文章的内容及语言表达进行最后的审读，剔除与主题不相干的语句，增强语言的精准性。这一步骤有助于学生提高写作质量以及养成良好的写作习惯。

（五）实施以学生为主体的过程性评价

高中英语新课标强调评价的主体是学生，提倡"建立以学生为主体、促进学生全面、健康而有个性地发展的课程评价体系"。高中英语新课标同时指出，评价应该将形成性评价和终结性评价相结合，关注学生的学习过程，引导学生监控和调整学习目标、学习方式等，发挥过程性评价促进学生学习的作用。因此，写作教学中必须加强以学生为主体的过程性评价，切实提升学生的自我反思能力、写作能力与学习能力。

1. 评价的主体是学生

学生是学习的主体，也是评价的主体。在写作教学过程中，教师应该指导学生参与讨论和确定写作评价的目标、内容和方式等，使评价符合学生的心智特征，以及写作教学目标、要求等，并帮助学生学习使用适当的评价方法和评价工具，开展学生自评、同伴互评。这样不仅有利于培养学生自我反思、自我调控和自我修正的能力，还可以促进学生相互交流与合作，以实现共同进步。

作为写作过程性评价的主要参与者，学生应参与评价标准的讨论和评价工具的制定，参与自我评价或同伴间的交流互评活动，在评价过程中发现、分析、修正写作中存在的具体问题。只有这样，学生才能真正把握写作的重点，使用和掌握写作技巧和技能，体验和感悟语言的力量，评价才能发挥其应有的促学作用。

2. 评价应贯穿于写作教学的各个阶段

写作是一个在构思、草拟、修改、编辑之间不断循环往复的过程，因此以学生为主体的过程性评价不仅仅发生在学生完成写作之后，而应该贯穿于写作过程的各个阶段，即计划构思、拟写草稿、修改文稿、编辑校订四个阶段，使评价活动成为写作过程的有机组成部分和促进各阶段教学的有效途径。

在各个教学阶段，评价的着力点应有所不同。在计划构思阶段，学生要完成写作提纲，评价内容主要围绕写作提纲是否体现了写作目的、读者意识、主旨内容和结构组织等方面；在拟写草稿阶段，评价的侧重点在于学生是否根据编写的提纲完成初稿，此外教师还可对学生写作过程中存在的问题加以提示和关注；在修改文稿阶段，评价的重点在于所写初稿是否达到了本次写作的要求，即通过评价发现问题并进行修正；在编辑校订阶段，学生通过校阅文章，从语法运用、标点符号、单词拼写、大小写等方面对文章进行修改。

3. 评价工具的设计与使用

恰当地使用评价工具可以要求帮助教师更好地实施以学生为主体的过程性评价。教师要结合写作教学的具体目标、内容要求和学生基础等，组织并指导学生一起制定切实可行的评价标准，设计适合教与学的评价工具，并运用于各阶段的写作教学。下面是几种常用的评价工具。

1）检查列表（Checklists）

写作教学中使用的检查列表是帮助学生进行对照、反思、核查的评价工具，有助于学生养成自我检查、自我修正、自我反思、自主学习的良好习惯，逐步提高写作能力。

检查列表通常围绕主题思想（ideas）、组织结构（organization）、语气态度（voice）、选词（word choice）、语句流畅性（sentence fluency）和常规语法（conventions）等方面。但是，检查列表设计的侧重点应该因不同的写作文体、写作要求和写作内容而有所不同。

首先，教师需根据不同文体的写作特点和写作要求设计不同的检查列表。下面以描述性文章、记叙文、议论文、说明文、应用文为例，简述如何根据不同的写作文体设计检查列表。

描述性文章以用生动、形象的语言描述人物、事物、景物为主，感官细节的使用是学生必需的写作技能，因此检查列表的要点之一是"Have you used proper sensory details in your description?" 此外，描写人物时需关注对人物外貌、性格特征或心理活动的描述，侧重点可以是"What is special about his or her physical appearance? Are his or her personality traits clearly specified? Have you used inner speech to describe his or her thinking?" 而描写景物时则应侧重景物的主要特点（如形状、颜色等）或描写顺序，如"In what order (space or time) can you describe the object clearly?"

记叙文以记叙、描写和抒情为主，检查列表应凸显这些要素。检查列表的问题可以是 "What is the event supposed to convey? Is your writing developed in the chronological order? Are your feelings and attitude suggested in your writing?"

议论文主要阐明观点与看法，检查列表应重点关注文章是否论点明确、论据充分、论证合理等，比如："What is your thesis statement? Are there enough supporting details to support your thesis statement? Have you developed your writing in a clear and logical way?"

说明文对客观事物的性质、特点、功能、过程等进行说明或解释，教师应围绕这些要求设计检查列表。如介绍某一甜品的制作过程，需关注 "Have you introduced the ingredients by means of classification? Are the steps of making the dessert clearly illustrated in order?"

应用文是人们在生活、学习、工作中为处理实际事务而进行的写作，其特点是实用性强。因此，检查列表的设计应特别关注写作目的、读者意识和语言得体性。如给某部门经理写投诉信，侧重点应是 "Who is the intended reader? Have you specified the problems of the product objectively and clearly? What compensation do you claim?"

其次，不同的写作阶段有不同的写作要求和侧重点，检查列表的设计也因此而不同。下面以记叙文为例，从写作的四个阶段简单说明。

（1）计划构思（Planning）

计划构思阶段要帮助学生明晰写作思路，包括确定写作主题、收集素材、选择内容组织方式等要点。因此检查列表着重帮助学生理解和掌握记叙文的写作要点，并能运用于后续的草拟和修改阶段。教师可以制定如下的检查列表：

Checklist for Planning

☐ What topic do you want to focus on?

☐ What is the theme of your writing?

☐ What are the main events and characters involved in your writing?

☐ How are you going to arrange and organize your writing?

☐ What feelings do you want to express through your writing?

（2）拟写草稿（Drafting）

拟写草稿阶段的检查列表要指导学生在计划构思的基础上草拟初稿，帮助他们进一步明确主题思想，选择有趣和有意义的素材并抒发情感，运用合适的写作手法组织编排，较快、较准地形成初稿。例如：

Checklist for Drafting

☐ Have you stated your thesis clearly?

☐ Have you used enough details to make your story meaningful and unforgettable?

☐ Have you used sensory details to make your writing vivid and interesting?

☐ Have you expressed your feelings?

☐ Have you organized your story in time order?

（3）修改文稿（Revising）

修改文稿阶段的检查列表要引导学生从内容、结构、语言等方面审视自己的初稿并加以修改，使文章主题突出，叙事生动、形象且有条理，并能给读者留下深刻印象。例如：

Checklist for Revising

☐ Is the beginning of your story attractive?

☐ What details do you add to highlight the thesis?

☐ What signal words of time order do you choose to organize the details?

☐ Do you express your feelings with a variety of specific words?

☐ Do you give your story an impressive ending?

（4）编辑校订（Editing）

编辑校订阶段的检查列表主要帮助学生规范文章的语言，检查并改正语法、拼写、标点符号、大小写等方面的错误。教师可以根据学生的基础和需求设计如下的检查列表：

Checklist for Editing

☐ Do you use correct verb tenses to describe the event?

☐ Are there any spelling mistakes?

☐ Do you use punctuation where necessary?

☐ Do you begin all your sentences with capital letters?

检查列表没有固定模式，教师须根据写作文体、写作阶段和学生的实际需求，围绕写作要求、内容、结构和语言设计检查列表，引导学生规范、高效地写作。

2）评价量表（Rubrics）

评价量表（rubrics）是判断与评价学生写作的标准或规则。评价量表可以帮助学生在写前做好准备工作，引导学生在草拟、修改等阶段进行自我评定和改进，适用于写作过程的各个阶段。

根据写作教程 *Write Source*（Kemper et al, 2005）一书，评价量表是评定写作等级的量表。评价量表可以从主题思想（ideas）、组织结构（organization）、语气态度（voice）、选词（word choice）、语句流畅性（sentence fluency）和常规语法（conventions）等六个写作特征（traits）对写作进行评价。评价等级分为六等，分别是6（amazing）、5（strong）、4（good）、3（okay）、2（poor）、1（incomplete）。师生可根据每一个等级的相关文字描述对写作的六个特征进行评价。以下是议论文写作的评价量表：

Traits\Grades	6	5	4	3	2	1
Ideas						
Organization						
Voice						
Word Choice						

（Continued on the next page）

Traits\Grades	6	5	4	3	2	1
Sentence Fluency						
Conventions						

以上表中关于主题思想（ideas）的评价为例，我们可以看到这样的等级描述：

Grade 6: The writer's opinion is very well defended and firmly convinces the reader.

Grade 5: The writing has a clear opinion statement and persuasive details to support the writer's opinion.

Grade 4: The opinion statement is clear and has most details to support the writer's opinion.

Grade 3: The opinion statement is clear but more persuasive details are needed to support the writer's opinion.

Grade 2: The opinion statement is not clear and persuasive details are needed.

Grade 1: A new opinion statement and supporting details are needed.

这些具体清晰的文字描述可以帮助师生准确地判断一篇文章的等级。

以上评价量表的评价内容全面，评价标准清晰，等级描述准确，有助于教师比较全面、客观、准确、高效地批阅作文，也可帮助教师发现学生写作中存在的问题并有针对性地提出指导反馈意见。此外，该评价量表也是学生在写作过程中进行自我评价和同伴互评的有效工具。学生可以根据评价量表的评价内容和等级描述去反思、评价、修改自己的写作。当然，对于不同的写作文体，评价量表中六个特征的具体内容也应该有所不同。

3）批改符号（Symbols）

批改符号是教师在批改学生作文时常用的书面评价方式。简单明了的批改符号有助于学生快速有效地理解教师所要表达的批改意见。教师可以与学生商定一些约定俗成的做法，让学生在知道符号所示意义的情况下了解自己写作的问题，及时进行自我修正。例如，C代表"连词（conjunction）错误"，P表示"标点符号（punctuation）错误"，sp代表"拼写（spelling）错误"，G表示"语法（grammar）错误"，ww表示"用词错误（wrong word）"，×表示"此处有错"，

/表示"应该删除"，┐表示"另起一段"，|表示"应该分开"，等等。

　　此外，教师也可用书面文字的方式进行评价。通过书面的交流沟通，对学生写作中的问题加以具体指导，对学生的点滴进步给予鼓励，激励他们学习写作的积极性和主动性，帮助他们树立信心，切实改进英语写作。

第二章 描述性写作（Descriptive Writing）

一、描述的定义（Definition of Description）[1]

Definition of Description

Description is like a photograph or a painting in words. The writer uses a careful selection of specific and concrete details to make a clear dominant impression on the readers.

描述就是用生动、形象的语言把人物、事物、景物等的特征和性质活灵活现地刻画或描绘出来，使读者如见其人，如闻其声，如临其境。描述作为一种表达方式，不但在叙事抒情类文章中被频繁运用，在议论文和说明文中也常被用到。

二、描述性写作的要点（Essentials of Descriptive Writing）

Essentials of Descriptive Writing

1. Know your purpose

2. Focus on a dominant idea

3. Base your description on observation

1. 明确描述目的（Know your purpose）

描述之前应该首先明确描述的目的是什么。不同的描述目的需要使用不同的描述方法，选取不同的描述内容。比如描述一个场景，可以是为了渲染某种气氛，也可以是为了帮助刻画人物的个性，还可以是为了表达作者的某种情感。

---

[1] 本章第一、第二部分作者为上海市徐汇区教育学院孟莎。

只有明确描述目的才能做到言之有物，才能写出发自内心的真情实感，使文章拥有自己的灵魂。

2. 突出描述重点（Focus on a dominant idea）

无论描写人物还是情景，成功的关键是把握并突出其特点。比如在描写一个人物时，首先应确定是要突出描写这个人的哪一个特点。在选择描述内容时，要精心挑选有助于表达这个特点的细节。如果写作时把所有想到的内容统统罗列在文章中，会使文章没有重点，枯燥无味。所以教师要指导学生学会在仔细观察的基础上，筛选材料，突出重点。

3. 描述基于观察（Base your description on observation）

描述要在细致观察的基础上，把观察到的内容细致入微地写出来。仅凭模糊的印象难以写出生动具体、真切感人的文章。要写好一段描述性文字，必须首先学会细致观察。观察时，既要远观，也要近看，总体印象和具体细节相结合。观察时还要注意变化角度，既要写出描述对象的特色，也要写出自己最深刻的印象和感受。

三、描述性写作的常用写作技巧（Basic Skills in Descriptive Writing）

Basic Skills in Descriptive Writing

1. Choose orders of description

2. Use sensory details

3. Use figures of speech

1. 选择描述顺序（Choose orders of description）[①]

在描述性写作中，描述通常是按一定的顺序展开的。教师可以指导学生以空间顺序、时间顺序或是重要性的次序来进行描述性写作。

在指导学生进行描述性写作前，教师需帮助学生明确写作的主题与目的。因为只有明确写作意图，才能对描述对象的细节特征作出精准筛选，并合理安排描写顺序，从而起到有效烘托主题的作用。

在选择与主题契合的重要细节后，教师可指导学生按照观察习惯对描述对

---

① 本部分作者为上海市宜川中学林泓、上海市光明中学施翎。

象进行描写。通常，描写可从整体到部分，由表面到内部，或是由形状、色彩到位置、结构。如果描写物体，其顺序可以是由上到下，由前而后，从左至右，或由主要部分到次要部分，由外部结构到内部结构等。当描写人物外貌时，则可先描述对人物的整体印象，再描述人物外貌的局部特征，也可先局部再整体。而采用移步换景的方法描写景物时，则需随着观察点的变换，对不断展现的新画面进行描述。

　　教师在指导学生学习描述顺序时，可以引导学生阅读范文，边读边思考并圈出段落中描述所用的关键词，体会描述顺序。

写作实践①

Task 1: Read the paragraphs below. Then, find the topic and underline the signal words indicating the order of description in each paragraph to figure out how the details are organized.

> **Teaching Notes**
>
> 　　本活动通过让学生阅读范文并完成相关任务，引导他们从具体案例中理解和感受描写人或物的要点及技巧。
>
> 　　Paragraphs 1–3分别是对地点和物体的客观描述。在教学过程中，教师可指导学生关注并学会运用介词短语或者表示次序的副词或动词短语，或者以移步换景的方式来进行有序的描述。Paragraphs 4–5描述的是人，运用了从整体到局部、从上到下的描写顺序。教师需让学生了解选择恰当细节并以合理的顺序进行描写对于烘托主题的重要性。

Paragraph 1

In the middle of the rectangular-shaped courtyard stood three magnolia trees all in full bloom. A little girl was hopping among them. Under one of the trees stood her parents who are keeping an eye on her. In front of another tree a young couple were posing for a picture. At one end of the courtyard a group of youngsters had gathered behind an artist painting a limb, while at the opposite end a few elderly men and women stood admiring the flowering trees.

Topic: *a courtyard* ②

Signal words: *in the middle of ..., at one end of the courtyard ..., at the opposite end ...*

---

① "写作实践"部分提供学生使用的任务单，请登录"世纪外语网"（www.centuryenglish.com），进入"下载中心"，搜索关键词"高中英语写作教学"获取配套教学资源包。

② 斜体部分内容为参考答案。全书同。

Way(s) to organize the details: *from the middle to both sides*

Paragraph 2

Mr. Cook, a renowned American historian, arranges the books on his bookshelves in a unique way. In the upper right-hand corner, there are books about the development of the early colonies in New England and the War of Independence. Right under them can be found books on the slave trade, the plantation system and the growth of the southern states. The left side of the shelf contains hundreds of books concerning subjects of the Westward Movement, Indian culture, the cowboys' contributions to American society and the Gold Rush in California.

Topic: *the way Mr. Cook arranges the books on his bookshelves*
Signal words: *in the upper right-hand corner ..., right under them ..., the left side of the shelf ...*
Way(s) to organize the details: *from the right to the left, from the upper part to the lower part*

Paragraph 3

We first crossed some catwalks below the road part of the bridge (the Sydney Harbor Bridge). I was glad I wasn't afraid of heights. Looking down through the catwalk I could see the ground 50 meters (164 feet) below! Next, we climbed the ladders leading up, up, up to the bridge's arch. Cars sped by on the road below. The wind blew more fiercely the higher we climbed. More and more of the city slowly came into view. Soon we were approaching the very top of the bridge! What a scene it was at the top! Clear, bird's-eye views of the city extended in all directions. Looking south we saw the city skyline, the famous Opera House and the ocean.

Topic: *the Sydney Harbor Bridge*
Signal words: *first ... below ...; Next, ... up to ...; at the top*
Way(s) to organize the details: *from the down part of the bridge to the top of the*

bridge and the sensory details change with the movement

Paragraph 4

On the stage stands a smiling clown. The clown's short yellow hair covers his ears but is parted above the eyes. The blue eyes are outlined in black with thin, dark lashes flowing from the brows. He has cherry-red cheeks, nose, and lips, and his broad grin disappears into the wide, white ruffle around its neck. The clown wears a fluffy, two-tone nylon costume. The left side of the outfit is light blue, and the right side is red. The two colors merge in a dark line that runs down the center of the outfit. Surrounding his ankles and disguising his long black shoes are big pink bows.

Topic: *a clown*

Signal words: *a smiling clown; short yellow hair; blue eyes; cherry-red cheeks, nose, and lips; broad grin; fluffy, two-tone nylon costume; the left side of the outfit; the right side (of the outfit); the center of the outfit; big pink bows*

Way(s) to organize the details: *from general impression to particular details, from the upper part to the lower part*

Paragraph 5

Agatha had a narrow, oblong face with angular cheekbones and a pointed chin. Her slit-like eyes were a clouded hazel, and her thinly plucked eyebrows were shaped into a deceivingly perfect arch that followed the slight curve of her eye. A long nose hooked over continually pursed lips, which were painted a bright red in an unsuccessful effort to mask their natural thinness.

Topic: *Agatha's facial features*

Signal words: *a narrow, oblong face; slit-like eyes; thinly plucked eyebrows; a long nose; pursed lips*

Way(s) to organize the details: *from general impression to particular details and the description is related to the overall feelings the subject brings out*

Task 2: Describe the following pictures.

Picture 1

Teaching Notes

　　本活动旨在帮助学生通过完成介绍一家书店的写作任务,学习运用合理顺序描述一个地方的写作技巧。教师在指导学生写作时,可要求学生先仔细阅读检查列表(checklist)。以检查列表为提示,关注图片中对于写作对象来说重要的细节,并以合理的顺序展开描写。在讲评范文时,教师也可充分利用检查列表来帮助学生了解文章是否描述得清晰、生动。

Directions: Introduce the layout of a newly-opened bookstore to parents.

Checklist

☐ Do I know my target readers while writing?

☐ Have I included all the details important to my readers?

☐ Have I based the description on a proper observation order?

☐ Have I included proper signal words to make the description clear?

A new bookstore is opened near our school. In it children of all ages can enjoy themselves.

Standing at the entrance between the two window displays, you can see two bookshelves on your left, exhibiting picture books and books for older children respectively, separated by an area where little children can play with puppets and soft animal toys.

Walk into the store and a reading corner can be spotted at the very end of the bookstore where readers can sit and enjoy their reading.

Next to the reading corner, there is another relaxing zone where elder children can do puzzles and play intellectual games there.

If you want to buy some books for your children, you can go to the cash register, just beside the relaxing zone and opposite the picture bookshelf.

Picture 2[①] ·············

Teaching Notes

通过描述图片的活动,让学生运用本部分的写作技巧。在学生提笔写之前,教师可先通过一些问题,引导学生关注图片的主题,图片中人物的关系和图片中与主题相关的细节。这样,学生在描述图片的过程中就可以按照重要性的次序来进行细节安排,从而更好地突显主题。

Directions: Describe the picture according to the following questions.

- What is the topic of the picture?
- Is there any person that is immediately noticeable in the picture?
- What is the probable relationship between the girl and people around her?
- What are the people around the girl doing?
- How do the people round the girl look like?

In the picture, a girl is learning to ride a bicycle. Beside her, her parents and grandma are running with worried looks, sweating. To her left is her father, who is telling her how to ride while to her right is her mother supporting the bike with a first-aid case on her shoulder. Behind the bike, her grandma is following her closely. By holding the bicycle the girl's parents and grandma are trying their best to protect her from falling and hurting.

---

① 该图出自 2003 年上海高考英语试卷作文题。

2. 运用感官细节（Use sensory details）[①]

1）视觉（Sight）

视觉描写通过视觉，勾画物体的外形（包括形状、颜色、质地等）或人物的外貌（包括容貌、衣着、神情、体型、姿态等）、动作，把描写对象"图画般"地展现在读者面前，是描述性写作中最常用的技巧。例如：

- The building is a magnificent structure with a square base and a round top.（外形）
- The Dutchman was six-foot, a great red-faced, hot-tempered trek ox of a man.（外貌）
- Sundown bloodied the horizon.（颜色）
- During rehearsals, to get what he wanted from his orchestra, he would sometimes stamp his feet, snap his baton and tear his store to pieces.（动作）
  （选自《英语（新世纪版）》高一第二学期 Unit 5 Arturo Toscanini）

2）嗅觉（Smell）

嗅觉描写通过对被描述对象的气味特征的描写，包括让人产生愉悦或厌恶的气味，让读者用鼻子去感知作者的情感。嗅觉描写既可以渲染气氛，又可以体现某个场景的特征。其次，嗅觉描写对于人物特征的描写也能起到画龙点睛的作用。例如：

- The air smelled of sea funk and overturned earth.（烘托气氛）
- She smelled as if she had sprayed on all the samples on the perfumery counter.（凸显特征）

3）听觉（Hearing）

听觉描写把各种特征的声音，如美妙的音乐，凸显人或事物特征的声音等通过生动的描述，直达读者耳中，让读者产生如临其境的感觉。在表现现场的

---

① 本部分作者为上海市奉贤区致远高级中学顾欢。

紧张、恐惧或欢乐气氛时，听觉描写常常能起到其他几种感官描写所不能达到的效果。例如：

- The receptionist's keyboard clicked, the water dispenser gurgled, and from next door came the hollow whine of the dentist's drill. （紧张气氛）
- I was about half way back when I heard two shots, followed by a dull slam a few seconds later. （悲伤气氛）

（选自《英语（新世纪版）》高二第一学期
Unit 5 Why did I Quit Hunting?）

- The door squealed open. （恐惧气氛）
- Chanting "Beijing! Olympics!" at the top of one's voice seemed the commonest means of expressing one's feelings. （欢乐气氛）

4）触觉（Touch）

触觉描写把人类最直接的体感表达出来，把物理环境、生理感受、物理特征等信息（如饥饿、疼痛、冷暖、软硬等）传达给读者，让读者通过作者的描绘，感受到文中的情感表达。例如：

- She groped her way through the darkness, her fingers sliding across sharp-edged stones and damp sticky walls.
- Her fingers skimmed the cool, silky water.

5）味觉（Taste）

味觉描写把所感受到的味道表达出来，在描写食物时是必不可少的。恰当的味觉描写可以调动读者的味蕾，让人仿佛亲口尝到了美味佳肴。此外，作者还可以"酸甜苦辣"味觉的描绘来比喻人生百味,这样也能感染到读者。例如：

- The coffee had that sharp-bitter taste of a too-often reheated brew.（食物描写）
- Life is full of sweet surprises. （其他对象）

写作实践

Task 1: Read the following paragraphs and underline the sensory details.

Teaching Notes

通过阅读范文寻找感官细节的活动，帮助学生从具体案例中理解什么是感官细节，体会感官细节对于描述性写作的重要作用。

(1) Moist① and salty②, a chilly breeze blows in across the waves, bringing with it the strong smells of seaweed and fish③ and making me pull my jacket a little closer. Sea spray transforms into fiery prisms④ as the waves splash against the shore, catch the last golden rays of sun, and toss them up like liquid crystals.

(2) There's beauty in the woods, too, especially late in the fall. Sometimes you walk among the huge trees, where the sunlight filters through. It's quiet⑤ and big, with touches of white and green and gold. And the silence is like that of a church.

(3) The playing field was a sea of red—all types of red outfits; from the skimpiest shorts to the most oversized T-shirts. The victory train had offloaded all its passengers there and they were jumping, chanting and waving red flags to the rhythm of the campaign song "Woy, Woy, Woy something's happening ..." Vendors had come out in large numbers to capitalize on this excellent opportunity to earn some extra income and the atmosphere was filled with attempting flavor of barbecued chicken and spare ribs, popcorn, roasted corn and plantains, grilled fish and other delicacies which were being lavishly consumed by the large and growing crowd. Alcoholic beverages were flowing freely; everyone seemed to be holding a bottle or a cup and the ground was littered with cups, plates and food wrappings. There was a cool breeze blowing from the sea, but it did very little for the sweating bodies on fire with the fresh, heady taste of victory. It seemed that everybody was there and the throbbing music and chanting voices could be heard from miles away.

---

① ____ : 触觉　② □ : 味觉
③ ～～ : 嗅觉　④ ____ : 视觉
⑤ ＝ : 听觉

Task 2: Use sensory details to describe a particular place or person.

描写地点（Describing a place）

Example 1

	Sight	Smell	Hearing	Touch	Taste
The summer beach	the blue sky, ...	fresh breeze, ...	the noise of the waves, ...	cool water, soft sand, ...	salty water, fresh, delicious seafood, ...
A park in early spring	*a host of little mild flowers (scattering), ...*	*scents of a carnival (blowing), ...*	*bird singing, ...*	*moist, cool, soft grass, ...*	*the sweet taste of spring*
Classroom	*the L-shaped classroom, inspiring slogans, the vigorous plant corner, ...*	*a mixture of various scents, ...*	*discussion, argument, chatting, laughter, either silent like a church or noisy like a teahouse, ...*	*teacher's encouraging pat on the shoulder, ...*	

描写人物（Describing a person）

Example 2

	Sight	Smell	Hearing	Touch	Taste
My mother	thick, long black hair, diamond-shaped face, ...	a slight scent of soap, ...	nagging, ...	rough hands, ...	

（Continued on the next page）

	Sight	Smell	Hearing	Touch	Taste
My best friend	*white skin, pink cheek, black eyes, long eyelashes, ...*	*fragrance of pineapples, ...*	*giggling, a silvery voice, ...*	*soft hands, silky skin, ...*	
An idol of mine	*well-built, muscular, barrel-chested, ...*	*smell faintly of sweat, ...*	*a deep and loud voice, ...*	*prickly beard, ...*	

3. 运用修辞手法（Use figures of speech）[①]

在中学英文写作中有时也需要运用一定的修辞手法。如果运用得当，会使文章增添文采。最常用到的有明喻（simile）、隐喻（metaphor）和拟人（personification）三种修辞手法。

Definition

A **simile** is a figure of speech that says that one thing is like another different thing. We can use similes to make descriptions more emphatic or vivid.

A **metaphor** is a fi ure of speech that says that one thing is another different thing. This allows us to use fewer words and forces the reader or listener to fi the similarities.

Personification treats animals and inanimate objects as if they were human with human characteristics. It enables readers and listeners to relate to animals and objects as they imagine them reacting or feeling the way a human would.

1）明喻（Simile）

把被比喻的"本体"和用以比喻的"喻体"同时说出，说明本体事物像喻体事物，

---

① 本部分作者为上海市徐汇区教育学院孟莎。

用介词like，连词as, as if, as/so ... as，动词seem等表示"好像"的意思。例如：

- My love is **like a red, red rose**.
- He smokes **like a chimney**.
- His muscles are **as hard as iron**.

2）隐喻（Metaphor）

根据两个事物间的某些共同的特征，用一件事物去暗示另一事物的比喻方式。本体和喻体之间不用比喻词，只是在暗中打比方。例如：

- America is **a melting pot** where new ideas are kindled.
- Art **washes away** from the soul **the dust** of everyday life.

3）拟人（Personification）

把无生命的事物或动物当作人来描写，赋予无生命之物以感情和动作或是把动物人格化。例如：

- My bicycle **is happy** to be washed.
- She did not realize that opportunity **was knocking at her door**.

写作实践

Teaching Notes

通过阅读范文找出作者所用的修辞手法，帮助学生学习和理解明喻、暗喻和拟人等三种修辞手法，体会修辞手法在描述性写作中的作用。

Task 1: Underline the figurative language used in the following paragraphs and tell what kind of figure of speech it is.

(1) What a scene it was at the top! Clear, bird's-eye views of the city extended in all directions. Looking south we saw the city skyline, the famous Opera

House and ocean. <u>It was just like looking at a postcard</u>①, except that we were really part of the picture!

(2) What happened next is hard to believe, but it's true. And it all seemed quite natural. <u>Just as when a friendly puppy comes near you</u>, I reached up and scratched his head, right between the horns. And he liked to be scratched. <u>That big, wild, beautiful deer bent his head like a young horse.</u> In fact, he practically asked for more. I scratched his head and his nose poked at my shoulder. He didn't even tremble.

(3) Mrs. Dursley was thin and blonde and had nearly twice the usual amount of neck, which came in very useful as she spent so much of her time <u>craning over garden fences</u>②, spying on the neighbors.

(4) <u>The woods are getting ready to sleep</u>③—they are not yet asleep but <u>they are disrobing and are having all sorts of little bedtime conferences and whisperings and goodnights.</u>

(5) It was a town of machinery and tall chimneys, out of which <u>interminable serpents of smoke</u> trailed themselves for ever and ever, and never got uncoiled. It had a black canal in it, and a river that ran purple with ill-smelling dye, arid vast piles of building full of windows where there was a rattling and a trembling all day long, and where the piston of the steam engine worked monotonously up and down, <u>like the head of an elephant in a state of melancholy madness.</u>

Task 2: Write a sentence using one of the figures of speech to describe the following people and things. Be original!

> the Great Wall   the Oriental Pearl TV Tower
> my brother   my dog   the clock

Teaching Notes

通过写句的活动，为学生提供初步运用明喻、暗喻和拟人等三种修辞手法的语言实践活动。答案是开放的，教师可以通过个人造句，班级交流的方式，激发学生的想象力。

---

① ___ : Simile
② ～～ : Metaphor
③ ＝ : Personification

(1) The Great Wall runs across northern China like a huge dragon. (Simile)

(2) Walking along the beach, we can see the Oriental Pearl TV Tower standing like a giant on the other side of the Huangpu River. (Simile)

(3) My brother likes to parrot what others say. (Metaphor)

(4) My dog always greeted me at the door when I came home. (Personification)

(5) The clock on the wall ticked loudly and lazily as if I had time to spare. (Personification)

第三章 记叙文写作（Narrative Writing）

一、记叙文的定义（Definition of Narrative Writing）[①]

> **Definition of Narrative Writing**
>
> Narrative writing is a piece of writing that recreates an experience through time, which can be based on one of your own experiences or of someone else. In addition to telling a story, a narrative writing also communicates a point to the readers.

记叙文是以叙事为主要表达方式，以记叙自身或他人发生的事情或经历为主要内容的一种文体。记叙文一般用时间顺序组织，通过记叙生动形象的事件反映生活，表达作者的思想感情。文章的中心思想蕴含在具体材料中，通过对人或事生动的记叙和描写来表现。

二、记叙文写作的要点（Essentials of Narrative Writing）

> **Essentials of Narrative Writing**
>
> 1. Centre around the topic in narrative writing
> 2. Involve the conventions of narrative writing
> 3. Employ elaborative details
> 4. Convey a point in narration

1. 围绕记叙的主题（Centre around the topic in narrative writing）

记叙文的主题是文章的"灵魂"。写记叙文应紧扣主题，特别是题目中呈现主题的关键词，并围绕主题选材和组织文章内容。选材时要挑选那些最能凸

---

① 本章第一、第二部分作者为上海市复兴高级中学楼蕾。

现主题、对作者来说重要、有意义和有感触的材料，这样才能使文章不偏离中心，表达作者的真情实感，打动读者。

2. 涵盖记叙文写作的要素（Involve the conventions of narrative writing）

记叙文写作包含以下基本要素：叙事背景（时间、地点、人物）、叙事人称（第一或第三人称）、情节（开端、发展、高潮、结尾）以及叙事顺序（顺叙、倒叙、插叙）。记叙文必须有一个主要事件作为"主线"，所有的细节都应围绕"主线"组织并为其服务。

3. 运用细节使记叙生动（Employ elaborative details）

记叙文写作应避免平铺直叙。如果只是将记叙的事件——简单罗列，文章就平淡而缺乏吸引力。在记叙过程中可以通过对人物、场景、对话、情感和心理活动等细节的描写以及设置悬念等修辞手法渲染、烘托记叙的事件，使文章更生动。

4. 记叙中升华主题（Convey a point in narration）

作者可以在记叙的基础上揭示、挖掘和提炼事件内在的深刻意义，发表感想或说明道理，实现主题的升华。

三、记叙文写作的常用写作技巧（Basic Skills in Narrative Writing）

Basic Skills in Narrative Writing

1. Use time order

2. Use descriptions

3. Use dialogues, inner speech and indirect speech

4. Use reflections

5. Use rhetorical devices

1. 运用时间顺序（Use time order）[1]

1）记叙的顺序

按时间顺序叙述是记叙文常用的写法。这种叙事方式可以帮助作者清晰地展开故事情节，也便于读者阅读理解。顺叙、插叙和倒叙是最常用的三种记叙手法。

---

[1] 本部分作者为上海外国语大学附属大境中学沈珊红。

（1）顺叙（Chronological order）

顺叙是按照故事发生、发展的先后顺序进行叙述的一种方式。顺叙的优点是叙事脉络清晰，是最常用的记叙手段。例如：

Sample 1

When my mother, at 16, after quarreling with her father, left his house on Dominica and came to Antigua, she packed all her things in an enormous wooden trunk that she had bought in Roseau for almost six shillings. She painted the trunk yellow and green outside, and she lined the inside with wallpaper that had a cream background with pink roses printed all over it. **Two days after** she left her father's house, she boarded a boat and sailed for Antigua. It was a small boat, and the trip would have taken a day and a half ordinarily, but a hurricane blew up and the boat was lost at sea for almost five days. **By the time** it got to Antigua, the boat was practically in splinters, and though two or three of the passengers were lost overboard, along with some of the cargo, my mother and her trunks were safe.

（选自 *The Circling Hand*, Jamaica Kincaid）

作者运用表示时间的短语或从句按事情发展顺序，记叙了从"我"的母亲决定离家及之后所发生的一系列事件。

（2）插叙（Narration interspersed with flashbacks）

插叙是指在记叙过程中，暂时中断叙述而插入与主要情节相关的其他情节。插叙可以为主要情节或中心故事做好铺垫和作补充说明，使情节更完整，内容更充实。但是插叙必须在顺叙的基础上进行，内容必须服务于中心故事，否则就会干扰故事主线的展开，影响读者的阅读。例如：

Sample 2

"Mimi, wake up. You are going to be late for school," my mom's voice cut through my dream.

I got slowly out of bed, dazed and disoriented. For a few moments, I didn't even know where I was. Then I remembered, and my dreams and memories came flooding back. **I remembered the long journey and the day after my cousin's death when we finally found land. We'd landed on a Malaysian island and stayed for sixteen months before being sponsored by St. Mary's church in Ohio. The Lord had answered all our prayers!**

Six years have passed, but I still occasionally have dreams about my long journey to America. I felt luck and grateful that we found land and a new life in America. I learned never to give up hope.

（选自 *Merlyn's Pen*, Van Ngo）

故事以主人公清晨被母亲唤醒开始，随后插入一段回忆六年前那场辗转赴美经历的内容，结尾段又回到现在。

（3）倒叙（Flashback）

倒叙是先交代故事的结局或某些情节，然后再回过来叙述故事的开头和经过的叙事方式。倒叙可以引起悬念，吸引读者阅读，增添文章的生动性。例如：

Sample 3

I caught sight of her at the play, so I went over during the interval. She addressed me brightly.

"Well, how time does fly! Do you remember meeting me the first time? You asked me to luncheon."

Did I remember?

It was twenty years ago and I was living in Paris, in a tiny apartment, and I was earning hardly enough money to keep body and soul together. One day I received a letter from her saying that she would like to have a chat with me about one of my books, so would I give her a little luncheon at Foyot's? Foyot's is a restaurant for French senators and it was far beyond my means. But I was pleased, and I was too young to have learned to say no to others.

So we met at Foyot's, on Thursday, at 12∶30 pm.

（选自 *The Luncheon*, William Somerset Maugham）

故事以男女主人公的再次相遇开篇，通过对话，尤其是男主人公的一句内心自问，引入20年前在他们之间所发生的一段故事。

2）使用表明时间的信号词

在记叙过程中经常使用表明时间的信号词，即具有时间意义的连接词，如before、after、until then、next、first、finally、in the meantime等，表示事情发生的时间顺序。使用这类信号词可以使故事发展的脉络更清晰，文章的结构更完整，也更方便读者阅读。例如：

Sample 4

When John Cowles and his wife and baby moved to Wisconsin in 1843, they built a one-room cabin to live in. All the cabin needed was a front door. **Until then**, they had hung a heavy quilt over the doorway.

John Cowles was a doctor. **One night before supper**, a messenger came for him. Someone was sick on a farm about twelve miles away. "I'll be home tonight or tomorrow morning," he told his wife. He quickly packed his things and rode off into the darkness.

His wife left a pot of beans simmering on the hearth in case he was hungry when he got home. **Then** she got into bed with her baby and went to sleep.

Sometime during the night, Mrs. Cowles awakened. She sensed that someone was in the cabin with her, probably her husband. But when she opened her eyes, she saw a bear in front of the fireplace. He was eating the beans, mouthful after mouthful.

Suddenly he stopped. He looked up and stared across the room at her. In the darkness, his eyes looked like burning coals. She wondered if he could see her. If the baby were attacked, what could she do?

> The bear turned back to the beans. **When** he finished with them, he pushed the quilt aside and left.
>
> （选自 *A Pot of Beans*, Alvin Schwartz）

suddenly 在此处有时间信号词的作用，引出后面发生的事情，增加了叙述故事的悬念和戏剧化的效果。

当我们在叙述一个故事时，必须先给故事确定一个时间框架（time frame），即故事何时开始，何时结束。所叙述的故事时间跨度可以在一天之内，小到几小时或几分钟，也可能是在几十年间甚至跨越几个世纪。我们可以借助图示或提纲，理顺故事的发生、发展顺序。

写作实践

Task 1: Read the passage and fill in the blanks with proper transitions.

> **Teaching Notes**
>
> 本活动旨在帮助学生学会正确使用时间连词表示故事发生和发展的顺序。

(1) When he returned an hour late   (2) Suddenly   (3) In a matter of seconds

(4) When I was five   (5) As   (6) Until the moment

_____(4)_____ we went to Yosemite for our first vacation. _____(5)_____ my mother and father sat outside the cabin reading the newspaper, I played near the river with the bear, dipping his furry feet into icy water. He was my best friend; I took him everywhere, could not fall asleep at night without him. _____(2)_____ the current swept him out of my hands. I ran screaming and crying to my father, "Daddy, hurry, Bear's gone down the river." _____(3)_____, he'd tossed his newspaper aside and followed me to the place where I last saw Bear. Leaping from boulder to boulder he seemed to be flying down the creek, his red flannel shirt billowing like a flag, finally disappearing from view. _____(1)_____, drenched and disheveled, he had Bear in his hands. _____(6)_____ I had never been conscious of loving my father. I wonder if he realized then just how thoroughly Bear had taken his place. And if he knew what a disaster it would be for both of us if he'd returned empty-handed.

Task 2: Read the following passages and identify what type of time order each passage uses.

Teaching Notes

本活动旨在帮助学生理解和识别记叙文写作中按照时间顺序记叙的常用手法。

(A)

Fortunately, I caught the plane to New York and everything seemed to have settled down. But only I myself knew what a frustrating and exciting experience I had early this morning, I almost missed the plane!

I arrived at the airport three hours in advance. Suddenly I was horrified to find that I had left one of my suitcases at the hotel. Without a second thought, I jumped into a taxi and explained my situation to the driver. Then we sped off towards my hotel ...

...

In the end, we managed to get the suitcase and then raced back to the airport. How lucky I was that I made it to my plane on time. (*flashback*)

(B)

My heart is full of excitement as Dad and I line up for this year's Charity Run. It is my first race. I've been working out and I feel so great. I know I'm ready. Bang! We're off. As we run side by side, Dad is panting, "Coop, don't forget ... how hard you worked ... to get here."

Yes. Dad and I had started training several months ago. Each day in our early morning walks, we'd go faster and faster. Slowly, the walks turned into jogging. Then they finally turned into running. At first, I had a tough time keeping up with Dad, so sometimes he would slow down for me.

...

Suddenly, I hear Dad panting beside me. He tells me to go on. So I take off like a racehorse roaring ahead. ... I sprint across the finish line. The big race clock shows 1 : 57 : 15. I feel so proud of myself! (*narration interspersed with flashbacks*)

Task 3: The following sentences are given in random. Underline the time order signal words in each sentence and rearrange them in chronological order. The beginning of the passage is given.

How would you feel if citizens of a rival town stole your town's records, forever changing its history?

(1) <u>Later one night that year</u>, some young Wheaton men broke into the Naperville courthouse and stole the county records.

(2) But these were destroyed in the Great Chicago Fire of <u>1871</u>. Wheaton has been the county seat ever since that famous midnight raid.

(3) In an <u>1867</u> referendum Wheaton narrowly won the county seat, but the records stayed in Naperville.

(4) An alarm sounded and they dropped some of the papers.

(5) In <u>1838</u> Naperville held the county records of the new Dupage County. Naperville and nearby Wheaton were fierce rivals. Both wanted the County seat.

(6) <u>Later</u>, fearing another raid, Naperville officials moved the remaining records to Chicago for safekeeping.

(5) — (3) — (1) — (4) — (6) — (2)

Task 4: Try plotting the events given below in your narrative in chronological order. Add things necessary to make it a good story. The beginning sentence is given.

1:30 p.m.   Ben and Paul set off riding their mountain bikes through the woods near their house.

4:45 p.m.   They felt confused when they came to a fork and took a wrong turn. They got lost.

9:00 p.m.　　They tried to keep warm and build a shelter with branches to spend a miserable night in the woods.

7:00 a.m.　　The next day, they continued to find the way back and saw old railroad tracks.

8:00 a.m.　　By following the tracks, they reached the town safe.

Ben and Paul were fond of cycling and one sunny afternoon, they decided to take an adventure across the woods near their house.

They set off at about 1:30 riding their mountain bikes. Everything went well until they reached a fork in the road. After thinking for a while, they chose the trail on the right, which, unfortunately proved a wrong way later. They got lost. It was getting darker and darker. Realizing it was impossible for them to find the way back, they collected some branches to set up a shelter where they spent a miserable night, cold and hungry. When they woke up early the next morning, they continued to find the way back. Luckily, they saw old railroad tracks, leading them out of the woods. It was nearly 10 hours before they got back home safe.

2. 运用描述 (Use descriptions)①

1）背景描述

在记叙文开头通常有一段简要的描述，交代事件发生的背景，主要是时间、地点、场景和人物。例如：

Sample 1

The Paris Opera House was a huge building. Beneath the building there was a strange, dark lake. On this lake was an island. On that island, one hundred years ago, lived the Phantom.

（选自《英语（牛津上海版）》高一第二学期

Unit 1 The Phantom of the Opera）

---

① 本部分作者为上海市复兴高级中学楼蕾、上海市崇明中学沈柳。

《剧院魅影》第一段简要介绍了故事发生的时间、地点和主人公。

2）细节描述

（1）行为动作

在记叙的过程中，作者可以通过使用动词描述行为动作，具体、清晰地呈现事件过程。例如：

Sample 2

The director **hurried down from** the control room opposite the stage. 'We need another contestant before the show begins,' he **shouted**. 'Who wants to be on TV?' Angela **raised her hand**. 'You are on!' the director **shouted**. After he **seated** her on the stage, a make-up artist **rushed forward**. She quickly **powdered** Angela's face and **combed** her hair.

（选自《英语（牛津上海版）》高一第一学期
Unit 4 Surprises at the Studio）

作者通过描述演播室里导演和其他工作人员一系列的动作展现情节的发展，渲染了演播室里紧张的气氛。

同时，作者还可以使用不同的动词使记叙更生动，人物刻画更鲜明。例如：

Sample 3

'No, let the fool wait,' **growled** Saleem. 'Business comes first.'

He **ordered** the engineer to press the button.

'Good, that's that. Turn it off. Now get that doctor in there,' he **commanded**.

'Where?' **demanded** the businessman, impatiently.

（选自《英语（牛津上海版）》高二第二学期 Unit 5 Green Orchids）

作者使用growl、order、command和demand等动词生动刻画了主人公专制、粗鲁和唯利是图的形象。

（2）心理活动

心理活动是指人物在一定环境中对周围事物和所发生的事情产生的看法、感触、联想等思想活动。人的行为、表情、语言等都受人的心理支配，因此在写记叙文时要发挥想象，动情描摹，把人物的内心感受揭示出来，使记叙生动，更具立体感。常用的描写心理活动的方法有直接描写、神态烘托、动作暗示、环境衬托等。

① 直接描写

直接描写是表达人物内心情感最常见的方法，通过作者介绍式的描述表现出来，常使用动词want、hope、wish、understand、realize、notice、feel、wonder等，直接呈现人物的心理活动；或用"be/get/become/seem+ 表语"句式描写人物的喜怒哀乐、惊讶、失望、激动、渴望等情感。例如：

Sample 4

In the Phantom's house, Christine pulled off his mask and saw the real man. At first, she **was shocked at** his horrible face with yellow eyes and no nose, but then she **felt sorry for** his suffering. She **understood** how lonely his life had been. She gently kissed his face.

（选自《英语（牛津上海版）》高一第二学期

Unit 1 The Phantom of the Opera）

作者运用这些词组直接描述了Christine见到Phantom撕下面具后从惊讶到同情再到理解的情感变化。

Sample 5

One evening, on their way to a distant university, Einstein said, 'I **wish** I didn't have to give my lecture tonight, Hans. **I'm so tired**, but I don't **want** to let my audience down.'

（选自《英语（牛津上海版）》高一第二学期 Unit 2 Two Geniuses）

动词wish、want直接表明了Einstein的愿望；be tired则写出了他当时疲惫的身心状态。

② 神态烘托

神态烘托指用能表达不同神态的动词引出说话者的内容，所选的动词都极具画面感，使读者可以通过这些动词准确想象说话者当时的神态和表情，从而准确揣摩人物的心理活动，了解人物的个性特征和内心情感。例如：

Sample 6

'Five minutes until we start filming,' **shouted** the director. 'Is everybody ready?'

'I'm glad that I'm not one of the contestants!' **whispered** Mandy. 'They must be worried now!'

...

'Oh, she's fainted because it's too hot,' **gasped** Mandy. A cameraman helped the woman off the stage.

（选自《英语（牛津上海版）》高一第一学期
Unit 4 Surprises at the Studio）

作者运用这三个动词分别形象地刻画了导演激动、兴奋的情绪和Mandy惊讶、紧张的情绪。

Sample 7

On discovering the error, I went back and tried to tell her. 'Excuse me,' I said. However, before I could continue, she **barked**, 'Can't you see there's a queue? Go to the end and wait your turn.'

（选自《英语（牛津上海版）》高一第二学期 Unit 5 What Should I do?）

由bark引出收银员的话语，形象地反映了她不耐烦的心理。

③ 动作暗示

动作是心理的外在表现，人物的心理通过动作向外界传达。在记叙文中对人物的肢体语言或富有个性的动作加以恰当的描写，能生动刻画出人物的内心世界，揭示人物的心理活动。例如：

Sample 8

Mandy, however, was tense. She **sat on the edge of her seat and chewed her fingernails** while she watched.

...

Mandy was so excited. She **could hardly keep still.**

（选自《英语（牛津上海版）》高一第一学期

Unit 4 Surprises at the Studio）

这两个动作生动形象地刻画出 Mandy 紧张、兴奋的心情。

Sample 9

The master **aimed a blow at** Oliver's head with his big spoon, **seized him tightly** in his arms and **shouted** for Mr. Bumble.

（选自《英语（新世纪版）》高二第二学期 Unit 7 Oliver Wants More）

作者运用这几个动词生动地刻画出当时统治者对待社会底层阶级冷酷无情的态度。

④ 环境衬托

环境衬托指对故事发生的环境进行恰当的描写，绘景而显情。借助环境或景物衬托人物的心理活动，既对刻画人物起到很好的作用，又能增添文章的意境，达到渲染主题的效果。例如：

Sample 10

The leaves fell slowly from the trees in the Square. Fell without wind. Autumn dusk. She felt a little sick.

...

Suddenly the lights came on up the whole length of Fifth Avenue, chains of misty brilliance in the blue air.

（选自 *Early Autumn*, Langston Hughes）

作者通过对树叶、黄昏、灯光、街道等不同景物的描写，生动细腻地烘托出女主人公起伏跌宕的感情波澜。

Sample 11

Colourful signs, loud music and exciting games attracted hundreds of visitors to a charity funfair at Rainbow School on Sunday. Earlier fears about the weather disappeared when the rain which had been forecast failed to appear.

（选自《英语（牛津上海版）》高三第一学期 Unit 1 Helping People）

本段借助环境的描写反映了作者对慈善义卖会的期待，预示着它的成功。

写作实践

Task 1: Choose the verbs from the box to complete the paragraph. Fill in the blanks with their proper forms and try to figure out what effects these verbs have produced.

> **Teaching Notes**
>
> 本活动旨在让学生用不同的动词准确描述主人公的行为并体会这些细节动作的描写所产生的效果。

> walk   see   smooth   decide   stop   thump   stick   knock

I (1) ____*saw*____ by the clock of the city jail that it was past eleven, so I (2) ____*decided*____ to go to the newspaper immediately. Outside the editor's door I (3) ____*stopped*____ to make sure my pages were in the right order; I

(4) ___smoothed___ them out carefully, (5) ___stuck___ them back in my pocket, and (6) ___knocked___ . I could hear my heart (7) ___thumping___ as I (8) ___walked___ in.

These verbs not only tell us what the storyteller did to meet the newspaper editor but also show us how important the meeting was for him and how nervous he felt.

Task 2: Find out the writer's feelings in the following passage and tell how the writer expresses his feelings.

> **Teaching Notes**
> 本活动旨在帮助学生熟悉并识别描写心理活动常用的几种方法。

My First Roller Coaster Ride

Last weekend I went to Six Flags in the state of Massachusetts. Six Flags is an American chain of amusement parks. It has many of the world's most amazing roller coaster rides.

Unfortunately, I am not a roller coaster person. I fear roller coaster rides so much that even a mild ride would make my legs shake[1] as if I had lost control of my muscles. My first roller coaster experience was not pleasant at all.

It was during the summer of 2010, in the city of Vancouver, Canada. I went to an amusement park with a group of friends. We were all very excited about roller coasters[2] and waited anxiously for the ride to begin. As the roller coaster went higher and higher, however, my heart started to beat so hard and fast that it seemed as if I could see my shirt move up and down. The laughter and the screams of my friends suddenly became very annoying. I just wished that they would all be quiet.

Then the big drop came. I closed my eyes and told myself that it would be over in two minutes. But it felt like a century and I was pushed up from my seat as if I were about to be thrown out of the roller coaster. By the time I finished the ride, I

① ____：动作暗示 ② ～～～：直接描写

could barely stand up and speak. I could only respond with silence when my friends asked me how I liked the ride. No matter how hard I tried, I could not make a sound.

Finally, the second voice won. I joined the line once again and emptied my mind of all worries. I kept my eyes open throughout the entire ride. I wanted to see what the ride was really like. I felt it a lot easier to have my eyes open. The drop no longer seemed frightening because I could see how fast I was going, and my mind was too busy savoring the wonderful scenery of the park to worry about fear.

3. 运用话语(Use dialogues, inner speech and indirect speech)[①]

1) 话语在记叙文中的作用

话语可以使记叙文的内容鲜活起来，常用来凸显人物性格，变换叙事顺序或故事场景，折射人物心理变化，直接呈现冲突或将故事情节推向至高潮。例如：

Sample 1

In the seventeenth round, Rivera, blown heavily, bent down. His hands dropped helplessly. Danny thought it was his chance-the boy was at his mercy. He decided to strike the deadly blow. But before he could do that Rivera caught off his guard and hit him in the mouth. Danny went down. When he rose, Rivera gave him another blow on the neck and jaw. He repeated this three times.

Danny did not rise again. The audience shouted for him to stand up. But the miracle did not happen.

"Count!" Rivera cried to the referee. When the count was finished, Danny, gathered up by his assistants, was carried to his corner.

（选自《英语（新世纪版）》高二第一学期 Unit 3 The Mexican）

如将最后一段改为 "Riversa asked the referee to count. When the count was finished, Danny, gathered up by his assistants, was carried to his corner.", 与原文比较可以看出，语言描写能更直接生动地描绘出在拳击场扣人心弦的厮杀气氛

---

① 本部分作者为上海市市北中学史海蓉。

下主人公的斗志。

Sample 2

Hit by a lack of fresh air, my head ached. Just as I tried to make the necessary adjustment to this new situation, Wang Ping appeared.

"Put on this mask," he advised. "It'll make you feel much better."

（选自人教版《英语 5》必修 Unit 3 First Impressions）

如将第二段改为 "He advised me to put on the mask and assured me that it would make me feel better. He handed it to me and immediately I felt better in no time.", 与原文比较可以看出，语言描写更生动地体现了在紧急情况下王平行动的果断。

Sample 3

I caught sight of her at the play, so I went over during the interval. She addressed me brightly.

"Well, how time does fly! Do you remember meeting me the first time? You asked me to luncheon."

Did I remember?

...

（选自《英语（新世纪版）》高三第一学期 Unit 5 The Luncheon）

此处作者用对话从 "与她久别重逢" 追溯到当年初次相见的情景。

Sample 4

His secretary asked whether she could bring the doctor in. The billionaire businessman made his decision.

'No, let the fool wait,' growled Saleem. 'Business comes first.' Despite

---

the health problems caused by his huge weight, he was still obsessed with making money. He raised a fat finger, and one of his staff hurried to switch on a large television set.

'Good, that's that. Turn it off. Now get that doctor in here,' he commanded. The doctor came in with a worried look and started to examine his wealthy patient.

（选自《英语（牛津上海版）》高二第二学期 Unit 5 Green Orchids）

作者通过对Saleem的语言描写表现了他傲慢自大、狂躁无理的性格及他的生活态度。

Sample 5

One day, uninvited, I went to her house, climbed up the hill, and a restless feeling grew within me at every step.

Margret almost jumped when she opened the door. She stared at me in shock. Then, quickly, In a voice I'd never heard before, **she said, "My mother says you can't come to my house anymore."**

（选自《英语（新世纪版）》高二第二学期 Unit 4 Adjo）

对人物的语言描写既反映出 Margret 的无奈，也折射出作者失望的情绪。

2）话语类型

（1）对话（Dialogue）

Sample 6

Einstein thought, 'Oh, no! Now we're in trouble.' But Hans just laughed and said, **'That's not a difficult question. In fact, it's so easy that even my driver know how to answer it. Hans, please ...'**

Einstein stood up and answered the question perfectly.

They left the university, with Einstein driving. A little later, Hans offered to drive. **'No, my friend,'** laughed Einstein. **'It's a pleasure to drive a genius like you, Hans.'**

（选自《英语（牛津上海版）》高一第二学期 Unit 2 Two Geniuses）

（2）内心独白（Inner speech）

Sample 7

Well, it wasn't much fun for me, and soon I went to sleep.

I must have slept pretty hard and pretty long. All of a sudden I woke up and could hardly breathe. Everyone was gone. The room was full of smoke! The house was on fire!

I started down the stairs and stumbled over a gray bunch. **"That belongs to Freckles,"** I thought. **"It's the gray sweater that he likes so much."**

（选自《英语（新世纪版）》高一第一学期 Unit 5 Well Done, Spotty!）

（3）间接引语（Indirect speech）

Sample 8

Luckily Mr Mandela remembered me and gave me a job taking tourists around old prison on Robben Island. I felt bad the first time I talked to a group. All the terror and fear of that time came back to me. I remembered the beatings and the cruelty of the guards and my friends who had died. I felt I would not be able to do it, but my family encouraged me. **They said that the job and the pay from the new South African government were my reward after working all my life for equal rights for the Blacks.**

（选自人教版《英语 1》必修 Unit 5 Nelson Mandela—A Modern Hero）

我们可以通过引号（"..."）以及一些有特征的动词来识别文中的对话或内心独白。除了常用动词ask、answer、reply、explain、command之外，对话通常由动词shout、cry、growl、murmur、whisper、gasp、blurt、smile、assure、threaten、promise、warn等引起。这些动词在引出对话的同时，还刻画了人物的动作、神态与性格特征。内心独白通常由动词think、wonder、hesitate、decide等引起。间接引语通常由动词say、tell、ask、explain、promise等引起。我们在写对话时应根据文章情节需要精心挑选动词。

在写对话时应注意：

① 词汇的选择：根据说话者身份、性格特征与想要描写的人物的心理和神情，选择适当的词汇（动词、形容词和副词）；

② 时态的正确使用：间接引语中的时态应该与所写文章前后时态呼应；而直接引语则应以说话的当时作为"现在"，时态使用以此为时间参照；

③ 在记叙与对话写作时注意人称的转换；

④ 注意引号内外的标点符号与大小写。

写作实践

Task 1: Mark the following dialogues with "D" and inner speech with "I".

> **Teaching Notes**
>
> 本活动旨在帮助学生依据对话和内心独白的不同特征对两者加以区分、辨识。

(1) The next day Ping Yu was leaving London for Windsor Castle. "Perhaps I will see the Queen?" she wondered as she fell asleep. (*I*)

(2) They began to talk about menus and balanced diets. "According to my research, neither your restaurant nor mine offers a balanced diet," explained Wang Peng. (*D*)

(3) "Wait till tonight," his friend whispered. "I expected there will be something about this on the television news. A real scoop!" (*D*)

(4) As Li Fang set off for home, he thought, "I guess Hu Jin doesn't love me. I'll just throw these flowers and chocolate away. I don't want them to remind me of her." So he did. (*I*)

(5) His cola was sugary and cold, and his ice cream was made of milk, cream and delicious fruit. "Nothing could be better," he thought. (*I*)

Task 2: Read the following sentences and fill in the blanks with proper forms of the verbs given below. Each verb can be used only once.

promise   smile   murmur   bark   answer   announce   tell   call out

(1) "That was very exhausting but very exciting too," I said. "Now I know much more about gravity! Do you think we could visit some stars next time?" "Of course," he *smiled*, "which star would you like to go to?"

(2) "Listen up, people!" he *barked*. "Welcome to the Warren Town Junior Drum and Bugle Corps. Being in a drum and bugle corps means you are alert and prepared at all times. Is that understood?"

(3) "Yes, sir," I *answered*, almost choking on the words.

(4) Mr. Carver follows me. He draws a deep breath and *announces*, "Our new home!"

(5) "I got you," Eric *called out*. "Swim back over and grab on."

(6) Whenever I face a challenging situation, I *tell* myself, "This will make a good story—if I ever get through it!"

(7) I looked at Luis and felt guilty challenging him since he was a good guy. "I'm really sorry about it, Luis," I *murmured*.

(8) Henry opened the car door and took a look at the boy lying on the ground. He tried not to let the man see how scared he was and *promised* he would do what he could.

Task 3: Read the two paragraphs and then fill in the blanks with dialogues according to the context. Try to make the paragraphs go smoothly and the description vivid.

(A)

One evening, my mom was downstairs doing the laundry. As usual, she was trying to do 10 jobs at once when she grabbed the wet clothes from the washer and tossed them into the dryer. She slammed the dryer door, turned the timer, and started to run upstairs. All of a sudden, a whining sound stopped her in her tracks. The sound was coming from the dryer. She yelled for me. (1) *"Oh, my God! That's terrible!/Oh, no! Something is wrong here!"* As I raced downstairs, the sound grew louder and louder. I flung open the dryer door. There to our surprise was Mica, our cat.

(B)

Dad used to be a thrill seeker. He enjoyed extreme sports like bungee jumping and rock climbing, and he took lots of careless risks. But one day, when he was riding his mountain bike, things got too extreme—even for him. It was a perfect day for riding. Once he reached the high point of the trail, he shot downhill. Suddenly, something jumped up in the path ahead of him. It was a black bear! (2) *"Take it easy. We're both scared."* dad thought to himself. Lifting his bike overhead, dad said in a deep voice, (3) *"Back, you! Back, bear!"* The bear stopped in its tracks and sniffed. Then it turned and ambled off into the woods.

4. 运用议论 (Use reflections)[①]

议论是指作者根据记叙的内容，融入自己的观点和评价，点明记叙内容的意义，以激起读者情感的共鸣。精彩的议论可以凸显文章的主题，升华事件的意义，真正起到画龙点睛的作用。议论部分的内容根据需要可以放在文章开头、中间或结尾。

1）以议论开头（Started with reflections）

在以议论开头的记叙文中，作者常常以富有哲理的语句作为开始，以此点明全文的主题，引发读者的思考；也常常通过发表感慨引出故事，激发读者的共鸣。例如：

Sample 1
Life is a series of choices, and we cannot always foresee the consequences.
Harry Saleem, an obese man with too much money and power, faced a

---

① 本部分作者为上海市崇明中学沈柳。

choice. Outside his office waited his personal doctor, bringing him vital news about the only medicine that could save his life. On the other side of the world, one of his engineers waited for his decision on an important matter of business.

（选自《英语（牛津上海版）》高二第二学期 Unit 5 Green Orchids）

作者在开头就点明了主题：人生就是一系列的选择，由此引出主人公因错误的选择导致无法挽回的结果的故事。

Sample 2

How the years have rushed by! It has been a long time since I knew Marget Swenson. I was a child when I knew her, and now I myself have children. **The mind loses many things as it matures, but I never lost Marget—my first love and first hurt.**

...

（选自《英语（新世纪版）》高二第二学期 Unit 4 Adjo）

开头的议论部分写出了作者的感慨和痛苦之情。她和 Marget 之间的友谊由于种族歧视而不幸夭折，给她留下了永远的伤痛。

2）中间插入议论（Interspersed with reflections）

作者可以在讲述故事的过程中插入议论表达看法、抒发情感，使读者能更深入地走进人物的内心世界，理解故事的内涵。例如：

Sample 3

...

The awful thing had come; my suspicion was confirmed: Marget was white and I was not. I did know it deep within myself.

...

（选自《英语（新世纪版）》高二第二学期 Unit 4 Adjo）

这段插在中间的议论反映了作者知道真相之后的忧伤之情。

Sample 4

...

It was a difficult decision to send a young woman, with neither a college degree nor scientific training on such a demanding task. Leaky had trust in her, but his colleagues predicted the young woman would fail. Goodall proved them wrong.

...

（选自《英语（新世纪版）》高二第一学期
Unit 5 Additional Reading Jane Goodall）

这段议论说明了作者对Goodall能完成去丛林研究黑猩猩这一艰巨的任务充满信心。

3）以议论结尾（Ended with reflections）

作者也常常在记叙文的结束部分通过发表对故事的看法或抒发情感的方式，引导读者进一步思考故事内涵。例如：

Sample 5

...

That moment will last in time forever. It expressed the whole meaning of the flame: love, enthusiasm, and brotherhood. It showed us all that love is really what makes this small world go around.

（选自《英语（新世纪版）》高二第二学期
Unit 4 Ryan, His Friends, and His Incredible Torch Run）

这段结尾的议论表明作者将永远铭记好友Ryan成为火炬传递者的时刻，从而升华了主题。

写作实践

Task 1: Read the passage and underline the reflection part which illustrates the theme of the story.

An Account of a School Activity

It was a bit chilly last night though it was already spring. However, on the playground in our school, you just felt hot and excited. Yes, the long-awaited show of the art festival finally would raise its curtain.

At about 7 p.m., the playground was already packed with audience. Seated in bright lights, we could see smiling faces everywhere. They talked and laughed as if they had never been so happy.

As soon as the hosts declared the show open, the performers beat the drums and the atmosphere reached its first peak. Throughout the show, we kept waving our light sticks, cheering and applauding. Our peers impressed us with their great talents and creativity. We just couldn't help feeling proud of them. How I wish I could be one of those who were standing on the stage, showing their youth and passion!

No doubt the art festival is a platform for us to display our talents. It is on this stage that we have the chance to fly our dreams and release our vigor. Please remember: give us a chance, and we are sure to return you a big surprise!

Task 2: Read the two passages and fill in the blanks with reflections.

Passage 1

A Bicycle Lesson

(1) *Parents are our first teachers. Up to now I still remember the "bicycle lesson" my parents gave me when I was only 7 years old.*

One day, my parents took a big bicycle and a mini one outside and taught me how to ride. Father jumped on his bicycle, showing me the way to ride a bicycle and mother kept telling me some basic skills. Then, it was my turn to have a try.

To be honest, I was very nervous. Touching the handle, I could feel my hands trembling hard and my heart beating fast. Noticing my nervousness, my parents smiled at me while saying something encouraging. It really took great courage for me to sit on the seat and move forward. Unluckily, I lost my balance, fell off the bicycle and skinned my knee.

"I would never learn to ride a bicycle!" I cried. My father came up and patted me on the shoulder, saying "Take it easy! Never say die before you finally do it! Try again and we'll be with you!" Though I failed several times, I finally succeeded with my parents' help and encouragement.

(2) *Father's words still echo around my ears now and then, giving me so much confidence and power in the course of my growth. From the "bicycle lesson", I have learned not only how to handle a bicycle, but also how to deal with the obstacles in life.*

Passage 2

A True Friend

When I was in Junior high school, Zhang was not a good choice to make friends with because he had dark skin and looked tough. I didn't like to play nor to talk with him, always keeping a distance between us.

One afternoon several young adults stopped me on my way home and bullied me into giving them some money. Just then, it was Zhang who stood out, shouted loudly and drove them away. I was very much moved when he came up and comforted me with a smile.

(1) *At that moment I suddenly realized how silly I was. I shouldn't have treated him that way.*

I began to watch him closely. Little by little, I found out he was a very nice boy, always ready to help others, whether classmates or strangers. He had a gentle heart under his dark skin and tough appearance. Of course we became friends finally.

(2) *From Zhang, I learned that sometimes appearance is misleading. Only by*

dropping our prejudice can we see the truth underneath and own friendship.

5. 运用修辞手段（Use rhetorical devices）

1）句子结构多样化（Vary sentence structures）[①]

在记叙文写作中尤其要注意变换句子形式。句子的多样性可以使文章上下文结构紧凑、意思连贯流畅、富有节奏感，避免单调乏味，增加吸引力。写作者可通过变换句子长度和句子结构使文章更具有文采。

（1）变换句子长度（Vary the length of sentences）

① 短句（Short sentences）

短句通常是简单句，有时甚至是省略结构。短句有助于清晰地表达一个意思。通篇连续地使用短句会使文章显得过于简单，但短句使用得当则能使文章节奏明快、描写流畅自然、各个动作环节突出、语言简练有力。例如：

Sample 1

Grandpa grinned; held out his hand in front of me. He snapped his fingers, out of blue, a quarter in his palm. Rapidly, he rolled his fingers and the quarter vanished. I'd seen this trick a hundred times, but today I was determined to figure it out.

② 中长句（Medium sentences）

中长句通常是指包含一个并列或主从结构的句子或带有少量修饰成分的简单句。中长句多用于叙事、展开情节和描写，为意义的衔接、细节的丰富提供了空间。在记叙文写作中较多使用中长句。例如：

Sample 2

Although I enjoy watching televised sports, I am often excited by the surprises that occur on the site.

---

① 本部分作者为华东师范大学第一附属中学姜振骅。

Sample 3

Instead of telling me his real name, he handed me a card with a simple sketch of a man with beard and one ear.

③长句（Long sentences）

长句通常包含两个或多个并列或主从结构的句子或带有多个修饰成分的简单句。长句多用于描写较复杂的情节、场景或刻画人物的心理活动。适当使用长句有助于强调一些无法断开的逻辑关系或添加重要、不可忽略的细节等，使描写流畅、完整、一气呵成。例如：

Sample 4

For over two decades, the Oriental Pearl TV Tower has stood at the entrance to Huangpu River, welcoming visitors from all over the world, immigrants from inner mainland and symbolizing the open and reform of the city.

Sample 5

The dancer, with the sleeves rolled up halfway, sat alone in the centre of the studio and kept his head down to let the sweat drip onto the floor, seemingly having no more strength to squeeze a fake smile.

（2）突出句子重心，保持句子平衡（Use front-loaded, end-loaded sentences and a balanced structure）

突出句子重心是指在记叙中有时为了突出句子主谓部分，引起读者注意，常常通过变换句子主谓部分的位置，将它们置于句首或句尾。记叙文中适当使用对称或平衡结构可以增加句子的平衡感和美感。

①重头句（Front-loaded sentence）

将句子主谓部分置于句首，后面紧跟着若干修饰短语，可给予读者人物的总体印象，侧重强调了人物的动作，并伴随修饰短语进一步细化。例如：

Sample 6

Dr. Lee is a typical economical husband, with thin appearance, big eyes and universal way of dressing.

Sample 7

He threw away the passport, determined never to come back to the country where his heart was broken by a women whose name he could barely remember.

② 压尾句（End-loaded sentence）

将句子主谓部分置于句末，为主要内容的呈现营造悬念。例如：

Sample 8

After having spent thousands of dollars and hundreds of hours decorating the apartment he loved, **Tony sold it.**

Sample 9

He turned the key in the lock slowly, sneaked into the room without breathing and gently put down the overcoat on the back of the chair; **all of a sudden, the light was on.**

③ 平衡结构（Balanced structure）

在句中使用平行对称的词、短语和从句可使句子对称、平衡并增加节奏感。例如：

Sample 10

Some have dreams about **flying, running** and **floating** while others about **drowning, restricting** or **imprisoning.**

Sample 11

We **dance like nobody's watching, sing like nobody's listening** and **live like it's heaven on earth.**

（3）变换句子开头（Vary the sentence beginning）

变换句子的开头是指将句子的某些部分，如副词、形容词、状语短语、非谓语动词、介词词组等置于句首，以强调行为方式、心理状态、时间方位等，与正常的语序相比更能体现作者所要描写的重心。多变的句子开头使文章句子呈现多样化，上下文衔接更加紧密，增加文章的吸引力和可读性。例如：

Sample 12

Eight o'clock in the morning, Li Hong was opening his jewelry shop for business. "I had a strange feeling that day," he said.

All of a sudden, a stranger entered his shop and stole three rings while Li Hong was getting some more rings out of the back of his shop. "It all happened so quickly," he added.

Running after the man, he tripped and fell over, pushing the thief to the ground too. Ironically, eyewitnesses said it was the best football tackle they had ever seen.

The thief went to prison and Li Hong got his rings back. We felt justice was done.

（选自人教版《英语 5》必修 Unit 4 Making the News）

Sample 13

Cautiously, the biologist approached the bird in the nest.（副词置于句首，强调人物的行动方式。）

Sample 14

On the wall hangs a well-elaborated clock.（将表示地点的介词短语提前，强调方位，突出描写，为读者提供视觉想象空间。）

Sample 15

Worried about his belongings, the monk placed them in a secret base. （将非谓语短语置于句首，强调人物忧虑的心态。）

（4）改变句子语序（Use inversion or emphasis）

记叙中适当使用倒装和强调结构可以突出句子的重心，增强句子的感染力。

① 倒装句。例如：

Sample 16

"On no condition should we tell him about it!" they agreed and moved on to the next station as if nothing serious had ever happened. **Never could they foresee** what to happen next would change their fate forever.

② 强调句。例如：

Sample 17

It was three minutes later that Teabing heaved a frustrated sigh and shook his head. "My friends, I am stymied. Let me ponder this while I get us some nibbles and check on Remy and our guest."

（选自 *The Davinci Code*, Dan Brown）

写作实践

Task 1: Rewrite the following sentences to emphasize the underlined parts.

> **Teaching Notes**
>
> 本活动旨在帮助学生掌握变换句子开头的写作技巧，以突出描述重点。

（1）I <u>fortunately</u> had begun my work on Thursday because the power failure on

Friday kept me from working on my paper.

Fortunately, I had begun my work on Thursday because the power failure on Friday kept me from working on my paper.

(2) The three puppies were <u>wet and dirty</u> when they rushed into the study.

Wet and dirty, the three puppies rushed into the study.

(3) She ordered a pizza <u>before she went to the store</u>.

Before she went to the store, she ordered a pizza.

Task 2: Improve the following passage by rewriting the sentences in brackets to make the narration natural and vivid.

> **Teaching Notes**
>
> 本活动旨在帮助学生在具体语境中根据上下文与情节需要正确并适当使用不同开头的句型。

A kitten, lost and found

Last Friday afternoon, as I returned home, I heard a strange noise. I looked around and found a kitten with a wounded leg lying in the corridor. (1) *Thin and hungry, the cat aroused my sympathy.* (*The cat was thin and hungry, and she aroused my sympathy.*)

I decided to take it home and look after it. (2) *Luckily, the kitten's leg was not badly damaged.* (*The kitten was not badly injured.*) I cleaned it and covered it with a bandage. I asked myself what else I should do.

The next morning, I wrote a notice about the kitten and put it on the notice board in my building. I hoped the kitten's owner would see it and contact me. Several hours later, a girl came to my home. (3) *"Oh, that is my baby cat!" she shouted excitedly, hugged the cat and kissed her.* (*She said that was her cat and she hugged her and kissedher.*) She told me that she had lost her pet on Friday and had just seen my notice. She thanked me for helping her pet. (4) *Never had I been that/so proud of myself because the little deed I did made such a big difference to others!* (*I felt proud of myself because the little deed I did made such a big difference to others.*)

2）设置悬念（Build suspense）[①]

悬念，一般指悬而未决的疑问，能让读者对故事中人物命运的遭遇和情节

---

① 本部分作者为上海市第三女子中学徐迪。

的发展变化产生一种急切期待的心理。悬念能使文章曲折生动，使读者不知不觉地进入文章所创设的情景之中。有时悬念设置在文章开头，有时设置在文章中间甚至结尾，是情节发展中不可或缺的一部分。设置悬念的方法有以下几种：

（1）提出修辞性问题（Raise a rhetorical question）

在写作时，作者可以通过提出疑问，迅速吸引读者的注意，引导读者继续阅读。但是提问之前必须交代产生悬念的前提，确保问题的有效性。好的问题既能引起读者注意，又能使他们保持注意力。在之后的叙事过程中作者必须解答疑问，使读者的好奇心得到满足，突出文章的主题。例如：

Sample 1

Susan was never interested in joining any group or sport during the summer. She figured that she got plenty of that during the school year. But then last summer, she saw a flyer for the Warrentown Junior Drum and Bugle Corps. She knew they were a very good group and got to travel a lot, so she decided to give it a try. Three months later, she said it was the best decision she had ever made. We were all curious about **what had changed her so much in such a short time.**

文中 what had changed her so much in such a short time 引起读者好奇。究竟是什么使主人公 Susan 在短短的时间内发生这么大的变化，这一问题也突出了文章主题。

（2）调整叙事顺序（Change time order）

除了直接提出问题，作者也可以通过合理调整叙事顺序来引发读者的疑问，设置悬念。作者可以不按照事情发展的自然顺序来写，而将故事的主要矛盾甚至结局放至文章开头，这样把最能表现中心思想的部分提到前面，不仅可以突出文章主题，而且能自然引发读者对事情发展过程的疑问，形成悬念。例如：

Sample 2

... 'It's all ready to blow, Mr. Saleem,' he said. 'Just say the word.'

> His engineer was standing above Pakan Valley in South America. **A few months ago, it had been a rainforest. Then Saleem's men had come ...**
>
> （选自《英语（牛津上海版）》高二第二学期 Unit 5 Green Orchids）

"It's all ready to blow ..." 和 "Just say the word." 给读者留下了疑问。在引起读者的阅读兴趣后，作者才将事情的始末娓娓道来，通过巧妙调整叙事顺序，成功设置了悬念。

（3）描述异常情景或意外事件（Describe extraordinary scenes or unexpected incidents）

在记叙过程中，作者还可以通过描述异常情景或意外事件引发读者疑问"为什么会这样？""突然发生了这样的事情，主人公会怎么解决？事情会朝什么方向发展？"这样的悬念可以位于文章开头，也可以位于文章中间，是故事发展必不可少的组成部分，也是使故事更加曲折、精彩的重要元素。例如：

Sample 3

The three contestants were sitting at their desks on the stage, waiting. ... **Suddenly, one of them, a woman, stood up and fell forward across her desk.**

（选自《英语（牛津上海版）》高一第一学期 Unit 4 Surprises at the Studio）

Sample 4

However, before Hans left the platform, a professor shouted from the audience, 'I'd like to ask you a difficult question.' He then asked a question so complex that Hans had no idea what he was talking about.

（选自《英语（牛津上海版）》高一第二学期 Unit 2 Two Geniuses）

在一篇好的叙事文章中，作者不仅要关注如何设置悬念，更要能够在悬念形成后，进行合乎情理地释疑。情理之中、意料之外的结尾往往能够使文章锦上添花，起到凸显人物性格、突出文章主题的作用。例如：

Sample 5

The day wore away, and even through the twilight they could see the lone ivy leaf clinging to its stem against the wall. With the coming of the night, the wind began to blow and the rain beat against the windows. When it was light enough the next morning, Johnsy, commanded that the shade be raised.

The ivy leaf was still there. ...

"Look out the window, dear, at the last ivy leaf on the wall. Didn't you wonder why it never moved when the wind blew? Ah, darling, **it's Behrman's masterpiece—he painted it there the night that the last leaf fell.**"

（选自 *The Last Leaf*, O.Henry）

维系着Johnsy生命的最后一片叶子最终是否会落下？在一连几天狂风暴雨后，这最后一片叶子为什么依然能够坚挺在树上？一个接一个的悬念在结尾处得到了解释——这片树叶是落魄画家Behrman用生命绘制的杰作。这一出乎意料却又合乎逻辑的结尾突出了小人物Behrman善良、博爱的品质和献身精神，点明了文章中心，升华了主题。

记叙文中，巧妙设置的悬念固然可以抓人眼球，使情节跌宕起伏，扣人心弦。但由于中学生刚刚开始学习英语记叙文的写作，所记叙的事情也往往较为简单，过度的悬念设置反而会过犹不及，显得故弄玄虚，因此建议适度使用。

▮▮▮ 写作实践

Task 1: Read the following passages and figure out how the authors build suspense.

Teaching Notes

本活动旨在帮助学生识别设置悬念的三种技巧，感受悬念对故事情节发展的推动作用。

(A)

Nearly a week passed before the girl was able to explain what had happened to her. One afternoon she set out from the coast in a small boat and was caught in a storm. Towards evening, the boat struck a rock and the girl jumped into the sea. Then she swam to the shore after spending the whole night in the water. During that time she covered a distance of eight miles. Early next morning, she saw a light ahead. She knew she was near the shore because the light was high up on the cliffs. On arriving at the shore, the girl struggled up the cliff towards the light she had seen. That was all she remembered. When she woke up a day later, she found herself in hospital. (*调整叙事顺序*。)

(B)

Our vicar is always raising money for one cause or another, but he has never managed to get enough money to have the church clock repaired. The big clock which used to strike the hours day and night was damaged many years ago and has been silent ever since.

One night, however, our vicar woke up with a start: the clock was striking the hours! Looking at his watch, he saw that it was one o'clock, but the bell struck thirteen times before it stopped. Armed with a torch, the vicar went up into the clock tower to see what was going on ... (*描述异常情景*。)

(C)

Late last summer, I was checking fences on my uncle's property when I smelled smoke. I looked up to see the hay field was on fire! Since I was the only one there, I had to do something. First, I hopped the split-rail fence and ran to the house. When I got there, I grabbed the phone in the kitchen and dialed 911.

"911. What's the nature of your emergency?"

"There's a brush fire just east of where Highway 9 crosses the White River!"

"Your name and address, sir?"

"I'm Andy Summers at 47113 Hammer Lane. When will you guys get here?"

"It'll take at least 10 minutes to get out to you. What I need you to do now ..."

"Oh man! The barn could be on fire by then!"

"Stay calm, sir. I need you to ..."

I hung up and called my uncle's cell phone. The phone rang four times before he picked up.

"This is Mark—"

"Uncle Mark! There's a fire——" I yelled, but his voice kept going.

"——Please leave me a voice-mail message after the beep and let me know where and when to call you back. Thanks."

After the beep, I said, "Uncle Mark! There's a fire in the hay field! I called 911 already, but get home quick!"

I hung up the phone and ran outside. I knew I had to do something on my own. If the tall grass around the stables caught fire, we could lose the barn, the stables, and even the house!

...（记叙不断出现的意外事件。）

Task 2: Build suspense in the following narration with the given requirements.

> **Teaching Notes**
> 本活动通过半开放的填空形式，帮助学生运用三种不同的技巧设置悬念，引起读者注意，为 Task 3 做好准备。

(1) Raise a rhetorical question.

At last firemen have put out a big forest fire in California. *But how did the fire begin?* Forest fires are often caused by broken glass or by cigarette ends which people carelessly throw away. But it was not the case this time. This morning, however, a fireman accidentally discovered the cause ...

(2) Use a different time order.

① A bird had snatched up the snake from the ground and then dropped it onto the wires. ② The snake then wound itself round the wires. ③ When it did so, it sent sparks down to the ground and these immediately started a fire. ④ When the firemen were trying to find out how the fire began, one noticed the remains of a snake which was wound round the electric wires of a 16,000-volt power line. In this way, he solved the mystery. ④①②③

(3) Describe possible extraordinary scenes or unexpected events.

At last firemen have put out a big forest fire in California. Since then, they have been trying to f ind out how the f ire began. Forest f ires are often caused by broken glass or by cigarette ends which people carelessly throw away. However, the firemen examined the ground carefully, but were not able to f ind any broken glass. They were also quite sure that a cigarette end did not start the fire. This morning a fireman accidentally discovered the cause. He noticed *the remains of a snake which was wound round the electric wires of a 16,000-volt power line*. In this way, he was able to solve the mystery. The explanation was simple but very unusual. A bird had snatched up the snake from the ground and then dropped it onto the wires. The snake then wound itself round the wires. When it did so, it sent sparks down to the ground and these immediately started a fire.

Task 3: Read the story and then rewrite it, using the skills you've learned to make it more suspensive.

> **Teaching Notes**
>
> 本活动要求学生利用所学技巧，如改变时间顺序、通过对话设问等，将一件平铺直叙的事件，改写成一个曲折生动的故事，帮助学生在具体写作活动中理解和掌握在记叙文写作中设置悬念的方法。

University students set the Embassy on fire this morning. The Ambassador of Escalopia was in his office when the fire broke out in the basement. He went down immediately and his employee Horst thought he was on fire and aimed a fire extinguisher at him, so his clothes got into a mess. In addition, someone fired a shot through the Ambassador's window and left a big hole on the hat, which he fortunately wasn't wearing. When he returned home for lunch, his wife was shocked that he looked so pale and the clothes were in such a frightful state. He told her the whole story.

When the Ambassador of Escalopia returned home for lunch, his wife got a shock. He looked pale and his clothes were in a frightful state.（倒叙+异常情景）

"What has happened?" she asked. "How did your clothes get into such a mess?"（通过妻子之口提出疑问）

"A fire-extinguisher, my dear," answered the Ambassador drily. "University students set the Embassy on fire this morning."

"Good heavens!" exclaimed his wife. "And where were you at the time?"

"I was in my office as usual," answered the Ambassador. "The fire broke out in the basement. I went down immediately. Of course, and that fool, Horst, aimed a fire-extinguisher at me. He thought I was on fire."（运用对话）

The Ambassador's wife went on asking questions, when she suddenly noticed a big hole in her husband's hat. "And how can you explain that?" she asked.（通过妻子之口提出疑问）

"Oh, that," said the Ambassador. "Someone fired a shot through my office window. Accurate, don't you think? Fortunately, I wasn't wearing it at the time. If I had been, I would not have been able to get home for lunch."（变换句子开头）

第四章　说明文写作（Expository Writing）

一、说明文的定义（Definition of Expository Writing）[1]

> **Definition of Expository Writing**
>
> In composition, expository writing is a pedagogical term for any form of writing that conveys information and explains ideas, also called exposition and informative writing.

说明文是一种以说明为主要表达方式的文章体裁。它通过对实体事物的科学解说，对客观事物做出说明或对抽象事理进行阐释。说明文具有内容基于事实、逻辑清晰、语言客观简洁等特点。在说明文写作中，常用手法有定义法、类比与对比法、过程分析法和因果分析法等。不同于描写文主要写外观和情感，记叙文主要写事件和经历，议论文主要在于"说服"，说明文所涉及的主要是阐述过程和关系。

二、说明文写作的要点（Essentials of Expository Writing）

> **Essentials of Expository Writing**
>
> 1. Clarify the purpose and target
> 2. Base the detailed content on the fact and evidence
> 3. Organize the information in a logical order
> 4. Write in brief, clear and objective language

1. 明确说明的目的与对象（Clarify the purpose and target）

说明文通过解释、介绍、阐述事物或事理的方式给人知识和信息，教人应

---

[1] 本章第一、第二部分作者为上海外国语大学附属浦东外国语学校徐宇琴。

用，帮助人们准确认识客观事物。针对说明的目的，被说明的对象不可太大也不可过多，说清楚是关键。

2. 基于事实的详细说明（Base the detailed content on the fact and evidence）

说明内容要实事求是，准确无误，要提供足够的实例和细节，将难以理解的抽象概念和需要解释探讨的各种问题说清楚。

3. 遵循逻辑顺序的内容组织（Organize the information in a logical order）

说明文中阐述的观点和事例应根据主题的性质，按逻辑顺序、时间顺序、空间顺序或认识顺序排列，条理要清楚，符合人们学习和掌握科学知识和有价值信息的认识规律。

4. 简洁、客观、清晰的语言表述（Write in brief, clear and objective language）

说明文写作中，语言要准确清晰，简洁明了，避免用华而不实的词藻或含糊不清的表述。

三、说明文写作的常用写作技巧（Basic Skills in Expository Writing）

Basic Skills in Expository Writing

1. Make a definition

2. Compare and contrast

3. Explain the process

4. Clarify cause and effect

1. 下定义（Make a definition）①

下定义是一种用简洁明确的语言对事物的本质特征作概括的说明方法，是说明文常用的写作技能。当我们说明一个具有多重含义，或者抽象、模糊或具有争议的术语或词语的时候，往往会使用下定义法对它进行限定，从而使其意义变得清晰。下定义有逻辑性定义和拓展性定义两种形式。逻辑性定义是基于词典解释的定义，用来说明某个具体的或没有争议的词语或术语，通常由术语（term）、分类（class）、特征（characteristics）三部分组成。拓展性定义主

---

① 本部分作者为上海市七宝中学黄岳辉。

要用来解释抽象和复杂的概念，它不是严格固定的，可以通过数字、举例、因果关系等信息作出清晰充分的解释。拓展性定义可利用分类（class）和特征（characteristics）来说明。

下定义类说明文写作过程中，通常在文章开头部分以逻辑性定义主题句的形式，说明某事物所属的分类以及它区别于其他事物的典型特征。在此基础上，以拓展性定义的形式，提供与主题密切相关的具体补充信息，使读者对该主题有更为深入的理解。

写作实践

Task 1: Read the following passage and fill in the form with the information you've got from the passage.

Friendship is a relationship of mutual affection between two or more people. Friendship is a stronger form of interpersonal bond than an association.

Although there are many forms of friendship, some of which may vary from place to place, certain characteristics are present in many types of friendship. Such characteristics include affection, sympathy, empathy, honesty, altruism, mutual understanding and compassion, enjoyment of each other's company, trust, and the ability to be oneself, express one's feelings, and make mistakes without fear of judgment from the friend.

While there is no practical limit on what types of people can form a friendship, friends tend to share common backgrounds, occupations, or interests. For example, in childhood, friendships are often based on the sharing of toys, and the enjoyment received from performing activities together.

Term defined	*friendship*
Class	*a relationship of mutual affection between people*
Characteristics	• *different in form with some common elements in different types* • *based on common backgrounds, occupations or interests*

Task 2: Read the following passage and tell the main idea and the function of each paragraph.

Teaching Notes

本活动旨在帮助学生通过阅读文章、小组讨论、归纳总结、完成表格进一步掌握说明文的基本结构和下定义类说明文写作的重点,即如何通过举例、解释等对主题作出清晰的说明。

Practical Jokes

A practical joke is a mischievous trick which is played on someone, generally causing the victim to experience embarrassment, confusion or discomfort. A person who performs a practical joke is called a practical "joker".

Practical jokes are generally lighthearted and without lasting impact; their purpose is to make the victim feel humbled or foolish, but not victimized or humiliated. In Western culture, April Fools' Day is a day traditionally dedicated to conducting practical jokes.

A practical joke is "practical" because it consists of someone doing something physical, in contrast to a verbal or written joke. For example, the joker who is setting up and conducting the practical joke might hang a bucket of water above a doorway and rig the bucket using pulleys so when the door opens the bucket dumps the water. The joker would then wait for the victim to walk through the doorway and be drenched by the bucket of water.

Practical jokes often occur inside offices, usually to surprise co-workers. Covering the computer accessories with Jell-O, wrapping the desk with Christmas paper or aluminum foil or filling it with balloons are just some examples of office jokes.

Paragraph	Main Idea	Function
1	*The logical definition of a practical joke*	*To give a clear definition*
2	*The general characteristics and purpose of practical jokes*	*To provide detailed information*
3	*The meaning of "practical" in practical jokes*	*To provide detailed information*
4	*The places where practical jokes often occur*	*To provide detailed information*

Task 3: Write a passage on "Happiness" in about 120—150 words. Your passage should include the following two parts.

a. Give the logical definition of happiness;

b. Provide some concrete information to help make the topic clearer to readers.

> **Teaching Notes**
>
> 巩固说明文写作的基本组成部分：术语、分类、特征。学生对"Happiness"的理解因人而异，写作过程中的重点是要提供具体例子来阐明自己对"Happiness"的定义。

Happiness

Happiness is a mental state of well-being or satisfaction, defined by positive or pleasant emotions. While some people think happiness has something to do with wealth and material success, others believe that it is closely related to positive emotions.

It goes without saying that material richness can bring happiness to us to some extent, but cases are often seen where many wealthy people fail to find the positive sides of their life and feel lonely, frustrated and even hopeless. Our life is full of ups and downs and we may face challenges like family breakup, academic failure in school, emotional hurt from friends, etc. But, as long as we always see the bright side of life even in the darkest days, we are sure to find the real and ever-lasting happiness in our life. So, keeping a positive attitude toward life is the right answer to gain our happiness.

2. 类比和对比 (Compare and contrast) [①]

在说明文中，类比和对比是一种常用的写作方式。作者通过选择的视角比较和对比两个事物，通过讨论两个事物的相似点或不同点，阐明具体问题，达到写作目的。一般来说，类比指出了同一类别中的两种或者多种事物的相似性，而对比则指出了事物之间的差异性。当然，在实际中，事物往往既有相似性，又存在差异性，所以类比和对比往往共同出现。在写作时，要选择恰当的视角，充分考虑目标读者，仔细分析类比与对比的方面，以具体的实例为依据，清晰地说明两者之间的相似点与差异。

---

① 本部分作者为上海市静安区教育学院汤华。

类比和对比的说明文写作技巧一般分为两种模式（pattern）:整体比较（the block pattern）和逐项比较（the alternating pattern）。整体比较时先讨论一项事物的各个方面，然后再讨论另一项事物的各个方面。而逐项比较时，按照比较项目展开，分项论述事物一和事物二。

类比和对比类说明文常用转换词连接类比和对比的二者，类比时常用both、each、at the same time、similarly、like、as、too、also、compared with等；对比时常用on the other hand、on the contrary、in contrast (with/to)、instead (of)、the opposite (of)、unlike、although、while、whereas、but、however、yet、nevertheless等。

 写作实践

Task 1: Read the following paragraphs and find out the objects and the aspects of comparison or contrast, the patterns and the ways used.

> **Teaching Notes**
>
> 　　通过阅读两段短文并完成表格，使学生具体了解和体会文本中类比或对比的对象、方面以及所使用的写作模式。

Paragraph 1

The same qualities that make people good house guests make them good hospital patients. Good house guests can expect a reasonable amount of service and effort on their behalf, and hospital patients can also. Guests have to adjust to what is for them a charge, and certainly hospital patients must do the same. No one appreciates complaining, unpleasant, unappreciative house guests. And the hospital staff is no exception. House guests who expect vast changes to be made for their benefit are not popular for long. Certainly nurses and other personnel with their routines feel the same way about patients in their care. Just as house guests must make adjustments to enjoy their visits, patients must make adjustments to make their stays reasonably pleasant and satisfying under the circumstances.

Paragraph 2

There is an essential difference between a news story, as understood by a newspaperman or a wire-service writer, and the news magazine story. The chief purpose of the conventional news story is to tell what happened. It starts with the most important information and continues into increasingly inconsequential details, not only because the reader may not read beyond the first paragraph but because an editor working on *galley proofs* (小样) a few minutes before press time likes to be able to cut freely from the end of the story. A news magazine is very different. It is written to be read consecutively from beginning to end, and each of its stories is designed, following the critical theories of Edgar Allen Poe, to create one emotional effect. The news, what happened that week, may be told in the beginning, the middle, or the end, for the purpose is not to throw information at the reader but to seduce him into reading the whole story, and into accepting the dramatic (and often political) point being made.

	Paragraph 1	**Paragraph 2**
Objects	*house guests and hospital patients*	*news story and news magazine story*
Aspects	• *amount of service and effort* • *adjustment to what is a charge* • *adjustments to make stays/visits pleasant and satisfying*	• *chief purpose* • *writing style and corresponding reading style*
Pattern	*alternating*	*block*
***Way*(写作方式)**	*comparison*	*contrast*

Task 2: Fill in the blanks to complete the passage with appropriate conjunctions.

> **Teaching Notes**
>
> 通过填词活动,让学生了解如何运用相应的连接词来完成类比或对比的写作。可能会有不同的答案,但是逻辑关系需表达清楚。

Even though Arizona and Rhode Island are both states of the U.S., they are different in many ways. For example, the physical size of each state is different. Arizona is large, having an area of 114,000 square miles, (1) *while/whereas* Rhode Island is only about a tenth the size, having an area of only 1,214 square miles. (2) *And/Besides, /In addition,* another difference is in the size of the population of each state. Arizona has about four million people living in it, (3) *but/while/whereas* Rhode Island has less than one million. The two states (4) *also* differ in the kinds of natural environments that each has. For example, Arizona is a very dry state, consisting of large desert areas that do not receive much rainfall every year. (5) *In contrast/On the contrary/Nevertheless,* Rhode Island is located in a temperate zone and receives an average of 44 inches of rain per year. In all, Arizona and Rhode contrast each other in many aspects and they are distinct from each other.

Task 3: Write a paragraph to compare or contrast "Eating" and "Reading".

> **Teaching Notes**
>
> 引导学生在段落写作实践中, 加深对于类比和对比的写作结构的了解, 学会选择和确定对比与类比的方面, 体验和运用此类写作方法。

1. Discuss and complete the following table from some aspects you may compare and contrast.

	Eating	**Reading**
Contrast	Meet the primary need of body	*Satisfy the intellectual need of mind*
Compare	Get basic nutrition	*Obtain information and knowledge*
	Enjoy the colour, smell and taste	*Relax and take it as a pastime*
	Avoid eating too much without digesting	*Avoid reading too much without understanding*
	Leave out the rotten part	*Reject the poisonous content*

2. Write at least two aspects of comparing or contrasting "Reading" and "Eating".

As a creature, I eat; as a man, I read. Although one action is to meet the primary need of my body and the other is to satisfy the intellectual need of my mind, they are in a way quite similar. To keep ourselves alive, we need to eat to take all kinds of nutrition. Having satisfied our hunger, eating can then be a kind of enjoyment. The colour, the smell, and the taste of the food are considered as important as its nutritional value. Similarly, to enrich our minds, we need information and knowledge through reading. Reading is one of the most important ways of learning. Sometimes, we take reading as a pastime, and meanwhile we relax and learn. Besides, there are other similarities between eating and reading. We should not eat too much without digesting, nor should we read too much without understanding. While eating, we should leave out the rotten part to maintain our health and while reading, we should be able to reject the poisonous content in a book so as not to poison our minds.

3. 过程分析(Explain the process)[①]

过程分析是说明文写作常用的一种写作技巧，一般分为指导性过程分析（directive process analysis）和知识性过程分析（informative process analysis)两种模式，往往以时间顺序描写一系列的动作和事件。撰写过程中，需要清楚地说明过程中的每个步骤，步骤间的关联，以及如何达到最后的结果。主题句要焦点集中，步骤的描写要清楚完整，步骤间的关联应清晰流畅，同时正确地使用过渡词，帮助读者理解。

写作实践

Task 1: Read the following passages and figure out the pattern of process and draw a flow chart for each to show the process.

Teaching Notes

组织学生以同伴互助的方式阅读并讨论两篇文本，了解文本的内容，判断过程分析使用的模式，并画出整个过程的主要步骤，从而理解两种不同类型的过程分析模式的特点，了解过程说明中常用的表示时间顺序的副词、短语或状语从句。

Passage 1

Saving a drowning person should take the following steps. First, place the victim on his back and remove any foreign matter from his mouth with your fingers. Then tilt his head backwards, so that his chin is pointing up. Next, pull his mouth open and his jaw forward, pinch his nostrils shut to prevent the air which you blow into his mouth from escaping through his nose. Then place your mouth tightly over the victim's. Blow into his mouth until you see his chest rise. Then turn your head to

---

① 本部分作者为上海外国语大学附属浦东外国语学校徐宇琴。

the side and listen for the out-rush of air which indicates an air exchange. Repeat the process ...

Pattern of process: *directive*

The process of saving a drowning person:

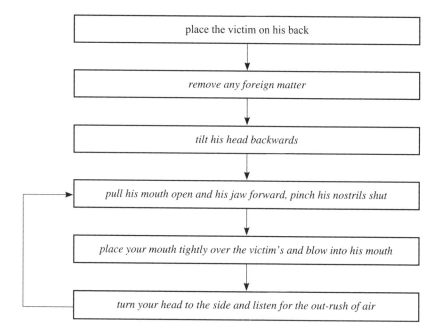

Passage 2

On arriving at the airport before traveling abroad, the first task is to check in your baggage on the flight. For this it is necessary to go to the desk of the airline concerned and hand over your luggage. The man at the counter checks both your ticket and your passport. He then weighs your suitcase and places it on the conveyor belt which will eventually take it onto your plane. When the flight is boarding, it is time to say goodbye to any friends or family who may have come to see you off. The traveler must then pass into the restricted area to go through immigration and a security check. Finally you climb the steps to board the plane. Once aboard and seated an air hostess comes round to make sure that you are wearing your seat belt properly. Now it is time to settle down and enjoy the flight.

Pattern of process: *informative*

The process of checking in at the airport:

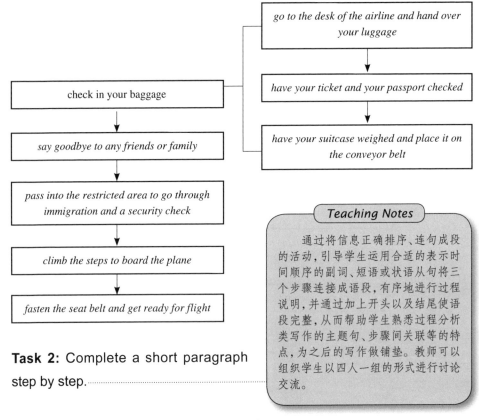

check in your baggage

say goodbye to any friends or family

pass into the restricted area to go through immigration and a security check

climb the steps to board the plane

fasten the seat belt and get ready for flight

go to the desk of the airline and hand over your luggage

have your ticket and your passport checked

have your suitcase weighed and place it on the conveyor belt

Teaching Notes

通过将信息正确排序、连句成段的活动，引导学生运用合适的表示时间顺序的副词、短语或状语从句将三个步骤连接成语段，有序地进行过程说明，并通过加上开头以及结尾使语段完整，从而帮助学生熟悉过程分析类写作的主题句、步骤间关联等的特点，为之后的写作做铺垫。教师可以组织学生以四人一组的形式进行讨论交流。

Task 2: Complete a short paragraph step by step.

1. Put the following steps in a proper order.

2. Combine them into a passage and add adverbs or adverbials of time if necessary.

3. Complete the paragraph with a beginning sentence and a concluding sentence.

How to improve/develop your study habit

(*2*) Make good use of time in class. Be sure to listen to the teachers carefully and take notes when necessary.

(*1*) Plan your time in advance. Remember to set aside enough time for preview before class.

(*3*) Review timely. Review important points mentioned in class as well as points you remain confused about.

Developing a good study habit is very important. The following steps can do *some help.* *(beginning sentence)* *First, plan your time in advance. Remember to* *set aside enough time for preview before class.* *Next, you should make good use* *of time in class. Be sure to listen to the teachers carefully and take notes when* *necessary.* *Then after class, review timely. Review important points mentioned* *in class as well as points you remain confused about.* *Having a good study habit* *cannot only ease your pressure, but also improve your study efficiency.* *(concluding* *sentence)*

Task 3: Complete the email, telling Granny how to start the WeChat and create a "family" group according to the pictures.

Teaching Notes

通过看图描述帮助学生操练过程性说明的技能,帮助学生掌握过程说明类写作的要求。教师在写作前可以让学生先看图口头描述过程,明确过程说明类写作的要求,如步骤的表达要清晰流畅、步骤间的衔接要自然、恰当使用过渡词等。

Vocabulary for reference

App store 应用商店	register 注册
log in 登录	icon 头像图标

Dear Granny,

I've heard that you are very much interested in WeChat. I'd be glad to tell you how to use WeChat to communicate with family members. Please take the following steps.

First, download the "WeChat" app, which can be found in App store. Next you can use your phone number to register and then set your name and ID. Right after you tap "+" in the top right corner and select "Group Chat", you can select contacts and click "OK" to start group chat. Then you can set the group name. Tap on the "people" icon in the top right corner, and click "Group Name". After you type in "family", the "family" group is ready.

Hope to chat with you in the "family" group soon.

Love,

Bob

4. 因果关系（Clarify cause and effect）[1]

因果关系的说明文主要描写事件、情况、行为发生的原因及结果。要写好一篇因果关系的说明文通常需要作者解释清楚事情发生的原因，透彻分析这些原因造成的结果，并将这些原因和结果在文中合乎逻辑地呈现出来。因果关系说明文写作一般分为三种形式：① 先陈述现象或后果，然后找出导致现象产生的一种或几种原因（the effect-to-cause pattern）；② 先陈述原因，后预测或解释由此产生的一种或几种不同的现象或后果（the cause-to-effect pattern）；③ 在一个段落中，描写的事物既是上文所述原因导致的结果又能成为导致后

---

① 本部分作者为复旦大学附属中学吴玮。

面某一现象产生的原因，即因果链模式（the causal chain pattern）。讨论原因的说明文通常在开头部分简单地交待结果，文章主体用来分析原因；讨论结果的说明文通常在开头部分交代原因，其余部分论述结果。

 写作实践

Task 1: Read the following passages to identify the cause and effect, and figure out what pattern each one belongs to. You can adapt the table if necessary. ⋯⋯⋯⋯⋯⋯⋯⋯⋯⋯

> **Teaching Notes**
>
> 本活动旨在帮助学生通过阅读认识因果关系类说明文的三种常见类型。教师可以在学生阅读后适当地进行提问，引导学生归纳因果关系类说明文的常见类型。

Passage 1

Obesity affects the individual and the country. The biggest effect is on the individual. First of all, being overweight has health risks. Obesity can lead to heart disease, diabetes, and other conditions. The quality of life suffers, as it is difficult to enjoy exercise or move. Another result is lack of self-esteem. This can lead to depression, eating disorders and crash diets. The country is also affected. It becomes very expensive for the government to provide advanced medical care such as heart transplants. Unhealthy citizens are also less productive and their children learn poor eating habits.

Topic sentence: *Obesity affects the individual and the country.*

The cause(s)	*obesity*
The effect(s)	• *health risks* • *lack of self-esteem* • *huge costs on medical care* • *less productive and poor eating habits of their children*
The pattern	*the cause-to-effect pattern*

Passage 2

There are a number of factors accountable for this situation that nowadays fewer and fewer students pay attention to their spelling. One of the most common factors is that fewer and fewer students need to write English essays. Besides, the goal of most students to learn English is to speak it and pass the examination, which means they just need to select the similar words according to the listening materials and passages. Perhaps the most contributing factor is the wide use of electronic devices such as e-dictionaries and computers and students no longer need to correct the words by themselves.

Topic sentence: *Fewer and fewer students pay attention to their spelling.*

The cause(s)	• *fewer students need to write essays* • *the changed goal to learn English for passing exams* • *the wide use of electronic devices*
The effect(s)	*less attention has been paid to spelling by the students*
The pattern	*the effect-to-cause pattern*

Passage 3

A family is one of the important parts of society, thus many people should be aware of the significance of couple relationship in family. Although people tend to think carefully before they get married, the rates of divorce continuously rise nowadays. At the moment, divorce has become the substantial problem because of women's changing roles, stress in modern life and lack of communication. Nevertheless, there are also the two different ways in effects, which are both negative and positive. Some couples, who have no children, divorce by consent, therefore divorce should be a good solution for couples to deal with this problem. On the other hand, other couples having children in their family should think deliberatively before they end their marriage in divorce; otherwise innocent children probably become victims for this situation.

Topic sentence: *The rates of divorce continuously rise nowadays.*

The cause(s)	• *women's changing roles* • *stress in modern life* • *lack of communication*
The effect(s)	*the rising rates of divorce*
The cause(s)	*divorce*
The effect(s)	• *divorce without children should be a good solution* • *children as victims of divorce*
The pattern	*the causal chain pattern*

Task 2: Write out possible causes or effects on the following designated topics.

Teaching Notes

本活动的目的在于帮助学生学会构建因果关系类说明文的基本框架。教师可以采用小组活动或同伴讨论的形式帮助学生激活思路,生成和主题相关的、符合逻辑的因果关系。

1. List three possible effects in Column "Effect(s)" for each of the causes in Column "Cause".

Cause	Effect(s)	
Overuse of mobile phone	Effect 1	*cause a bad influence on nervous system*
	Effect 2	*result in headache and decreased attention as well as depression*
	Effect 3	*harm eyesight*
Peer pressure	Effect 1	*make wrong decisions/adopt good habits*
	Effect 2	*cause psychological problems/cultivate competitive awareness*
	Effect 3	*lose identity/be better exposed to the world*

2. List three possible causes in Column "Cause(s)" for each of the effects in Column "Effect".

Cause(s)		Effect
Cause 1	*deforestation mainly caused by the cutting down of trees*	Global warming
Cause 2	*greenhouse gases given off by vehicles*	
Cause 3	*overpopulation*	
Cause 1	*reading books for a long time/in the sun*	Short-sightedness
Cause 2	*not having sufficient outdoor activities*	
Cause 3	*lacking enough nutrition*	

Task 3: Write a cause-and-effect paragraph by choosing one of the following topics. Before you start, you may first list some causes and effects that are associated with your topic.

Teaching Notes

本活动旨在引导学生独立思考,写出一个在结构和意义上都完整的因果关系的段落。教师可以通过开展"头脑风暴",运用"思维导图"或列提纲等活动帮助学生激活思路,并选择与话题相关的内容。

Topic 1: Some people choose to have a pet, because ...

Topic 2: Some people choose to have a pet, but ...

CAUSES for having a pet	EFFECTS of having a pet
1. A desire for companionship	*1. Causing harm to the environment*
2. To reduce stress	*2. Transmitting/Spreading diseases*
3. To advoid boredom	*3. Resulting in biting and attack*

1. *Some people choose to have pets because some pets, for example, dogs can comfort them while their family members are not in company with them. Many elderly people, for instance, like having a dog instead of being all alone at home. Pets can also help their owners relieve stress. When you go home after a long day of work, feeling exhausted and stressed, there is the adorable animal so happy to see, and then the stress will go away. Preventing boredom is another important reason to keep pets. Pets need a lot of attention. It's a nice way to spend one's time on them.*

2. *Some people choose to have a pet but they have never expected the serious consequences it will bring about. The abandoned animals by their irresponsible owners may pose great health risks to the city residents. They may also disturb the neighbours and make a mess of the sidewalks or even cause an accident because of their mischievous behaviour or excessive manure. Sometimes the pets may hurt the people who want to be close to them. In extreme cases, pet attack can actually kill people. Keeping a pet is, to some extent, harmful and risky.*

第五章　议论文写作（**Argumentative Writing**）

一、议论的定义（Definition of Argumentation）[①]

> **Definition of Argumentation**
>
> Argumentation is the process of forming reasons, justifying beliefs, and drawing conclusions with the aim of influencing the thoughts and/or actions of others.

　　议论是语言表达方式中常见的一种，它要求论点明确、论据充分、论证周密。议论是一种评析、论理的表述法。一段或一篇完整的议论，通常由论点、论据和论证三要素组成。

　　议论的特点是用说理的办法，以案例、事实、数据等形式，直接对客观事物进行分析、评论、表述观点，去影响和说服他人。

　　议论文是以议论为主，作者直接阐明自己的观点和主张的常用文体。它不同于记叙文以形象生动的记叙来间接地表达作者的思想感情，以事感人，也不同于说明文侧重介绍或解释事物的形状、性质、成因、功能等，以知授人，议论文则是以理服人。

二、议论文写作的要点（Essentials of Argumentative Writing）

> **Essentials of Argumentative Writing**
>
> 1. Establish clear and definite arguments
> 2. Apply sufficient and reliable evidence
> 3. Provide proper and strict demonstration

---

① 　本章第一、第二部分作者为上海市市西中学张芸。

1. 论点鲜明确切（Establish clear and definite arguments）

论点是作者对所论述问题的见解和主张，是议论文的灵魂。一篇议论文通常有一个中心论点，当然有的议论文还围绕中心论点提出几个分论点，用来补充和证明中心论点。论点一般在开头提出，然后加以论证。注意提出的论点一定要鲜明而确切，是作者看法的完整陈述。

2. 论据充分可靠（Apply sufficient and reliable evidence）

一般以事实、数据、案例等为论据，也可以利用谚语、格言等作为论据。论据必须充分可靠，用于论事说理。

3. 论证严密得法（Provide proper and strict demonstration）

议论文中的论点和论据是通过论证组织起来的。论证是运用论据来证明论点的过程和方法，是论点和论据之间逻辑关系的纽带。

归纳法（induction）和演绎法（deduction）是议论文常用的论证方法。归纳法以例子为基础，从数个例子和现象中，归纳出某种道理或看法。归纳时要注意使用的例子要充分可信，不能以偏概全。演绎法以一个或多个看法为基础，从一般论断，演绎到不同事例，再加以论述，最后再回到论断。

三、议论文写作的常用写作技巧（Basic Skills in Argumentative Writing）

Basic Skills in Argumentative Writing

1. State arguments clearly

2. Use evidence adequately

3. Develop paragraphs logically

1. 展开议论（State arguments clearly）[①]

展开议论需要合理搭建篇章的结构，而合理的篇章结构取决于文章的逻辑是否清晰，是否具有说服力。一般说来，我们通过在引言段（introduction）阐明观点，在主体段（elucidation）对观点加以论证，在结论段（conclusion）重申或强调观点的方式展开议论。

---

① 本部分作者为上海市长宁区教育学院张珏恩。

通常情况下，引言段必须简单解释要讨论的主题，一个清晰简练、亮出中心论点的主题句（thesis statement）一般会出现在该段的末尾句中。主体段是议论的过程，必须有足够的分论点（points）来论证观点，一般可以提出两到三个分论点，分别展开阐述，并辅之以充分的证据。结论段中要画龙点睛地重提自己的看法、意见或建议，必须要与引言段呼应，但不能照搬原话，也不能在此时出现任何新的信息。一般来说，议论文的每段应该有一个主题句，使读者对每段的主题一目了然。整篇文章展开时一定要注意段落间的有机联系，即在引言段、主体段和结尾段间应有使行文逻辑清晰的过渡词语或转接句（transitions）。

展开议论除了上述最常见的先提出观点，而后从几方面阐明观点，最后得出结论的方式（即 Introduction—Elucidation—Conclusion，也就是我们常说的"总—分—总"式）外，还有先提出论点，然后从几个方面论证的方式（即 Introduction—Elucidation，也就是"总—分"式），或先剖析所要论述的几个方面，然后综合归纳出结论的方式（即 Elucidation—Conclusion，也就是"分—总"式）。

写作实践

Task 1: Read the following three passages and find out the method of presenting arguments, the thesis statement and points of each passage. Underline the transitional words in each passage.

> **Teaching Notes**
>
> 通过阅读三篇文章及完成相关任务，帮助学生了解三篇文章的论证方法、寻找中心论点、论据和过渡词，同时关注议论文的行文结构，了解适时亮出观点并以充分的论据进行论证的重要性。

Passage 1

Letter Writing is Vital

Nowadays, with the development of science and technology, it seems that mobile phones and computers are taking the place of letter writing. However, I don't agree with this idea. In my opinion, letter writing is of great importance.

In the first place, letter writing has a long history. Since letter writing is one of the most valuable treasures of people, it is sure to last forever. People are used to writing letters to express their ideas and emotions, which is the reason why it is not easy to get rid of it.

In the second place, considering the fact that China is still a developing country, there are still many remote areas where people cannot contact others by mobile phones or computers but by letters. Without letter writing, how can they keep in touch?

In the third place, as for me, mobile phones and computers are so familiar to us that we won't be thrilled to receive a text message or an email sent by others. On the other hand, the excitement of receiving letters from friends is beyond description. While reading letters, I will feel specially happy and excited.

In a nutshell, letter writing is vital to all of us. Since most people are unaware of the importance of letter writing, it is high time to take measures to solve the problem. As long as we all pay great attention to letter writing, it will be bound to boom in the near future.

The method of presenting arguments: *Introduction—Elucidation—Conclusion*
Thesis statement: *Letter writing is of great importance.*
Points: *Letter writing has a long history.*
    Without letter writing we cannot keep in touch with people living in remote areas.
    The excitement of receiving letters from friends is beyond description.

Passage 2

Are Cartoons Good or Bad for Students?

Have you ever read cartoons? If you have, you are certain to lose yourself in them. Cartoons do give us a lot of amusement but is reading cartoons harmful to us students?

Some people think cartoons will affect students' study. This is right because there are many examples where some students' school performance becomes worse and worse resulting from cartoons. However, others argue cartoons help students develop their imagination.

Every side has a proper reason, but in my mind, cartoons are both the "devil" and the "good" in a way. With too much pressure on them, students feel tired and they just want to have a rest for a while. Cartoons are such a means to relax themselves. However, if they get too addicted to cartoons, they will lose everything. What's more, students learn something more quickly from cartoons than from textbooks because cartoons are what they are interested in. They will acquire some knowledge from cartoons that they may not get from their textbooks. But there is also something bad in cartoons, so students should learn to choose what they should read and what they shouldn't.

<u>In one word</u>, in spite of the advantages and disadvantages of cartoons, students' self-control is most important.

The method of presenting arguments: *Elucidation—Conclusion*
Thesis statement: *In spite of the advantages and disadvantages of cartoons, students' self-control is most important.*
Points: *Cartoons will affect students' study.*
Cartoons help students develop their imagination.
Cartoons are both the "devil" and the "good" in a way.

Passage 3

My Opinion on the Donation from the Shanghai Tobacco Group

The news that the Shanghai World Expo Bureau rejected the donation of 200 million yuan from the Shanghai Tobacco Group has swept over the nation. From my perspective, it brings a lot of benefits to the public.

<u>On one hand</u>, the purpose of the Shanghai World Expo is to create a pure, green, healthy and civilized atmosphere. The decision of the Expo Bureau not only promotes the idea of a smoke-free environment, but also maintains the international image of Shanghai before the public and its status throughout the world.

<u>On the other hand</u>, it is a must for the World Expo Bureau to take on the social responsibility and make good use of this opportunity to keep people from smoking. If the WEB had accepted the donation at that time, it would have been a negative influence on teenagers. So the bureau has made a wise decision and projected a responsible image.

The method of presenting arguments: *Introduction—Elucidation*

Thesis statement:*The rejection from the Shanghai World Expo Bureau brings a lot of benefits to the public.*

Points:　*The decision not only promotes the idea of a smoke-free environment, but also maintains the international image of Shanghai.*

　　　　It is a must for the World Expo Bureau to take on the social responsibility.

Task 2: Read the outline of "Letters won't Disappear". Pick out the point(s) you don't think support the thesis statement and improve it/them. Put a tick or a cross or write "To be improved" in brackets.

> **Teaching Notes**
>
> 　通过甄别所给分论点是否能支持中心论点并加以改进的活动,帮助学生进一步领悟分论点与中心论点的关系,并提高他们根据中心论点选择和确定分论点的写作技能。教师可组织学生展开讨论,产出更多好的分论点。

Letters won't Disappear

Thesis statement: Writing letters in pen will not be replaced by text messages or emails.

Points:

(1) The handwriting of the senders can bring you intimate feelings. 　　　　　($\sqrt{}$)

(2) Writing letters in pen is a convenient way to express your emotion. 　　　　($\times$)

Because it's also convenient to express your feelings through text messages or emails.

(3) The letters can be your fortune not only at present but many years later as well.

(*To be improved*)

Because letters here need to be defined clearly. 改为：*The letters written in pen can be your fortune not only at present but many years later as well.*

Task 3: Work out an outline according to the instructions given below in Chinese.

> **Teaching Notes**
>
> 　本活动旨在帮助学生运用和巩固展开议论时谋篇布局的基本技能。在列提纲前,教师可以引导学生就该作文题目展开深入的讨论,让学生通过"头脑风暴"形成观点,找到支持观点的分论点,并搭建起文章的框架结构,为之后的议论文写作打下基础。

　　在上海乘坐地铁需要接受安检(security check),但是有些乘客并不配合,请你谈谈对此现象的看法。

Security Check, Welcomed or Not?

Thesis statement: *The present situation is not the passengers' fault but the lack of overall consideration.*

Points: *The number of passengers has been overlooked.*

The training for metro workers is neglected.

...

Conclusion: *The local authority should revise its strategies for the sake of passengers' feel and convenience.*

2. 使用论据 (Use evidence [examples, statistics and facts] adequately) [1]

写议论文时,在提出主论点(thesis statement)和分论点(point)后,需要使用相关、充分且可靠的论据作支撑,使自己的主张或见解更具说服力。论据即论证的理由或依据,中学英文写作中较常用的有案例(examples)、数据(statistics)、事实(facts)等。教师在教授学生使用各类论据的同时,需要引导其关注并掌握不同的话语标记语(discourse markers)[2],并能运用这些话语标记语引出论据。此外,教师还应指导学生在使用论据时能够有意识地呼应分论点,从而使论据更好地起到支撑作用。

1) 列举案例(Use examples)

作者可基于个人的阅读、经验或亲身经历列举单一或多个相关案例,然后明确并阐释其属性,即:案例阐释了什么意义,从而呼应论点,形成直观而具体的支撑。例如在下文中,作者在主论点 "... there are still some reasons why manually changing the natural appearance is acceptable." 下提出了分论点 "Plastic surgery should be welcomed for medical purposes.",并用 "One of the examples ... is ..." 和 "Another example is ..." 引出案例作支撑,进而使用 "it is effective in ..." 和 "helps return a patient back to ..." 等语句使论据呼应论点。

Sample 1

Is Plastic Surgery Acceptable?

Though the significance of beauty in the modern world can be debatable,

---

① 本部分作者为上海市教育委员会教学研究室周杰、上海南汇中学周惠英。

② 话语标记语广泛存在于各门语言中,用以标记话语层次,在语篇中起着停顿、过渡、指示与提示等作用,有助于形成语篇的连贯性与条理性。

and there exist reasons against plastic surgery, **there are still reasons why manually changing the natural appearance is acceptable.**

...

Plastic surgery should be welcomed for medical purposes. One of the examples of such surgery is a lift in the eyes and around the forehead for those suffering from physical shortcomings; it is effective in reducing eye pain and headaches. **Another example is** surgery for damage received as a result of an accident-chemical burns, deep scars, and so on. Plastic surgery, in these cases, helps return a patient back to his or her original condition.

...

2）援引数据（Use statistics）

作者可基于个人的知识和经验积累或通过其他途径搜集、援引相关数据，然后解读并分析其内涵，即：数据说明了什么问题，从而呼应论点，形成客观而有力的支撑。例如在下文中，作者在主论点 "... students should not be allowed to use their cell phones or tablets at school, not to mention during classes." 下提出了分论点 "Prohibiting cell phones has a positive impact on students' academic performance.",并用 "According to a British research ..." 和 "it is discovered that ..." 引出数据作支撑，进而得出结论 "The ban on the use of cell phones contributes to students' academic improvement at various levels." 以呼应论点。

Sample 2

Should Students Be Banned from Using Cell Phones at School?

A cell phone today is a portable computer allowing its owner to deal with various tasks almost anywhere and anytime. Apart from this, a cell phone provides numerous entertainment options, which are especially favoured by the younger generation—high school students, in particular. Although a cell phone is already seen as a must for a teenager, yet **students should not** be allowed to use their cell phones or tablets at school, not to mention during classes.

...

Prohibiting cell phones has a positive impact on students' academic performance. According to a British research into cell phone policies in Birmingham, London, Leicester and Manchester schools, **it is discovered that** the schools that banned cell phones showed a sharp increase in test scores by 6.4% with few changes to other factors. The gains were observed among students with the lowest achievements, and among average ones, the results even doubled at 12.8%. The ban on the use of cell phones contributes to students' academic improvement at various levels.

...

3）陈述事实（Use facts）

作者可基于个人的观察和了解陈述客观事实或情况，然后探究并还原其本质，即：事实蕴含了什么道理，从而呼应论点，形成直接而有效的支撑。例如在下文中，作者在主论点 "Considering this, they should not be allowed for teens to play." 下提出了分论点 "Violent video games encourage violent behaviours."，并用 "As a matter of fact ..." 引出事实作支撑，进而使用 "Teenagers ... are well likely to be misled into taking violent action." 等语句使论据呼应论点。

Sample 3

Should Teenagers Be Allowed to Play Violent Video Games?

Times when children would spend their free time playing with peers in the streets have mostly gone. Modern children and teenagers prefer calmer forms of entertainment, such as watching TV, or playing video games. Although video games can contribute to a child's development, many of them, unfortunately, are violent. **Considering this, they should not be allowed for teens to play**.

105

...

Violent video games encourage violent behaviours. As a matter of fact, they do not only allow players to punch or kill virtual reality characters of other players, but also grant them with scores for successful acts of cruelty. Sometimes, players will even be praised verbally and directly, after conducting a cruel attack or killing. Teenagers may recognize the favourable feedback and, if they are not self-conscious enough, are well likely to be misled into taking violent action.

...

📚 写作实践

Task 1: Read the following paragraphs and fill out the forms that follow.

Teaching Notes

该活动旨在让学生尝试辨识分论点、论据类型、论据内容、引出论据的话语标记语,以及作者在构建论据与论点间联系时的分析等。

在此过程中,学生若遇到困难,教师可通过一些引导性的问题给予一定的支持。

Paragraph 1

Attending single-sex schools contributes to students' academic performance. According to a study conducted in Australia among 270,000 students, 88% of them, both male and female, showed better results in tests when attending separate schools. In an experiment held in Virginia in 2005, 10,000 k—12 graders were separated while studying STEM courses, and 96% of the girls were reported to have become more active, confident, and achieve better results. The majority of the students seemed to benefit from this approach, and it proved favourable for girl students learning STEM courses.

Topic	Should Boys and Girls Study in Separate Schools?
Point	*Attending single-sex schools contributes to students' academic performance.*
Type of evidence	*statistics*
The evidence	*270,000 students, 88% of them; 10,000 k—12 graders, 96% of the girls*

(Continued on the next page)

Discourse marker(s)	*according to; in an experiment held ...*
Analysis	*The majority of the students seemed to benefit from this approach, and it proved favourable for girl students learning STEM courses.*

Paragraph 2

Gap-year travelling makes students more sociable. Take myself as an example: I used to be shy and afraid of communicating with others. But travelling does open up windows for communication, as I have a lot of tourists sharing similar, if not the same, interests and purposes on the team to talk with. It even pushes me to contact others sometimes, as I need to ask for service in a restaurant; or I ask for guidance when I get lost. That makes me more outgoing and ready to engage in interactions.

Topic	Should Students Travel During a Gap Year?
Point	*Gap-year travelling makes students more sociable.*
Type of evidence	*examples*
The evidence	*I used to be shy and afraid ... when I get lost.*
Discourse marker(s)	*take ... as an example*
Analysis	*That makes me more outgoing and ready to engage in interactions.*

Paragraph 3

Being friends with students will somehow affect the teacher's authority. In fact, the teacher-student relationship is commonly built on a not-the-same level basis: students recognize their teacher as an outsider with the power or right to give orders, make decisions, and keep order. But teachers' becoming Facebook friends with students make them personally acquainted with each other and develop a close relationship beyond class. The familiarity may lead to the confusion of identity, which makes it difficult for teachers to discipline and reason with students.

Topic	Should Teachers be Facebook Friends with Students?
Point	*Teachers are not supposed to be Facebook friends with students.*
Type of evidence	*facts*
The evidence	*In fact, the teacher-student ... beyond class.*
Discourse marker(s)	*in fact*
Analysis	*The familiarity may lead to the confusion of identity, which makes it difficult for teachers to discipline and reason with students.*

Task 2: Think about the given topic, discuss the questions below with your partner and then make an outline for writing. ·····················

> **Teaching Notes**
>
> 通过讨论问题完成写作提纲的活动引导学生尝试围绕话题选择立场、思考主论点、分论点、论证策略等，由此初步形成论证思路。教师可将问题链印制成任务单，在课堂上先以互动问答的形式演示论证思路的形成过程，然后再要求学生独立完成提纲。

Topic: Should Students Wear School Uniforms?

Questions

(1) Which side will you take? Please set out your thesis statement.

(2) What will be one of your points under the thesis statement?

(3) What type of evidence will you use to support your point?

(4) What will the evidence be mainly about? Please briefly explain it.

(5) What discourse marker(s) will you use to introduce the evidence?

(6) In what way is the evidence related to your point?

Outline:

Thesis statement: *I am against making school uniforms compulsory for students.*

Point: *Forcing students to wear school uniforms is unfavourable for mental development.*

Type of evidence: *facts*

The evidence: *Students experience a growing need to be unique and special. Dressing is one way of showing different personalities.*

Discourse marker(s): *As a matter of fact, ...*

Analysis: *Students are robbed of a chance to express themselves. Students feel oppressed for being unable to show how different they are.*

Task 3: Write one paragraph in 60 to 80 words on the given topic with a clearly stated point supported by facts, examples or statistics.

> **Teaching Notes**
>
> 　　该活动旨在让学生在论证段落的写作中综合运用所学技能。写前，教师可组织学生围绕话题展开"头脑风暴"以激活思维，然后根据学生提出的论点和分论点，通过一些提示性的问题，适当启发他们调用已有知识或利用相关资源，查询收集事实、案例或数据等论据作支撑。

Topic: Should Leather and Fur Clothes be Banned?

Sales of leather and fur clothes will reduce some rare species to extinction. According to a research conducted by People For The Ethical Treatment Of Animals in 2013, it takes up to 80 mink skins to produce just one coat; each year, over 2,000,000 minks are being killed in animal farms for commercial purposes. It is regarded as the primary reason for the decreasing number of the species worldwide. Threatened with human desire for luxury and profits, they are dying out.

4）区分观点与事实（Tell opinions from facts）

观点指作者对某件事情的看法，带有明显的主观性。观点表达个人看法、判断、信念、态度、价值观等，常表现为推论、预测、结论等各种主观表达方式，不同的人有不同的看法与观点，如："Einstein's theories have a significant effect on the world."。事实指客观发生的可以被证明的事情，包括姓名、地点、日期、数据、事件、规律等，如："Gravitational waves were detected 100 years after Einstein's prediction."。

以下面的句子为例：

The price of the book is $20.	The book is too expensive.
Mr. James said, "I am a strict teacher."	Mr. James is the strictest teacher.
According to the research, using a cell phone while driving is dangerous.	Using a cell phone while driving should be banned.

从上表可以看出，表格左栏的句子都是事实，表格右栏的句子都是观点。"The price of the book is \$20." 是事实，而 "The book is too expensive." 则是对于书本价格的看法，是因人而异的观点。"Mr. James is the strictest teacher." 表达了对Mr. James的看法，是观点；但 "Mr. James said, 'I am a strict teacher.'" Mr. James本人这样说就是个事实了。

在议论文文体写作教学中，常常容易混淆观点和事实。因此，有必要指导学生区分观点和事实，以便在写作中正确地进行表达。

写作实践

Task 1: Read the following sentences and find out which of the following sentences are facts and which of them are opinions.

> **Teaching Notes**
>
> 通过本活动帮助学生区分观点和事实，并发现表示观点的常用表达方式，如：I believe, I think, I argue, I hold the belief that ...，等等。

(1) We have to admit that the way you say something is far more important than what you say. (*Opinion*)

(2) The shop assistant greeted the well-dressed lady in a cheerful way. (*Fact*)

(3) Some people like watching TV at home better than going to the cinema. (*Fact*)

(4) I think that maintaining eye contact in conversation is very necessary. (*Opinion*)

(5) I firmly believe that body language is of great importance in communication. (*Opinion*)

(6) Everyone wants to be heard, but very often people prefer to talk rather than listen. (*Fact*)

Task 2: Read the following passage and fill in the table.

> **Teaching Notes**
>
> 通过阅读范文和填写表格，帮助学生了解文章的结构，作者的观点，以及用于支撑观点的事实。

Security guard, truck driver, salesperson—year after year, these jobs appear on lists of the unhappiest careers. Although many factors can make a job depressing—unusual hours, low pay, no chance for advancement—these jobs stand out for another reason: a lack of small talk. Actually small talk can make people feel happy.

First, small talk could promote bonding. Chatting with strangers could brighten our morning. In a series of experiments, psychologists gave Chicago commuters varying directions about whether to talk with fellow train passengers—something they typically avoided. Those told to chat with others reported a more pleasant journey than those told to do whatever they normally would.

Besides, small talk can also help people feel connected to our surroundings. People who smiled at, made eye contact with and briefly spoke with their Starbucks *baristas*（咖啡师）reported a greater sense of belonging than those who rushed through the transaction. Similarly, when volunteers broke the silence of *the Tate Modern*（英国泰特现代艺术馆）to chat with gallery-goers, the visitors felt happier and more connected to the exhibit than those who were not approached.

Therefore, go ahead—small talk needn't be idle, and nosiness isn't all bad.

The writer's opinion	*Small talk can make people feel happy.*
Facts	• *Those told to chat with others reported a more pleasant journey than those told to do whatever they normally would.* • *People who smiled at, made eye contact with and briefly spoke with their Starbucks baristas reported a greater sense of belonging than those who rushed through the transaction.* • *When volunteers broke the silence of the Tate Modern to chat with gallery-goers, the visitors felt happier and more connected to the exhibit than those who were not approached.*
Conclusion	*Therefore, go ahead—small talk needn't be idle, and nosiness isn't all bad.*

Task 3: Pick out the facts from the sentences given below to support the opinion.

Opinion: There's no doubt that obesity has a negative effect on people's health.

Teaching Notes

本活动旨在指导学生学会选择与主题句相关的事实为依据支撑观点。教师可以指导学生通过抓住观点中的核心信息"肥胖对于健康的消极影响"来选择适切的事实依据。

Supporting facts: *(1), (5)*

(1) According to the World Health Organization, being overweight has now overtaken being underweight as one of the world's leading causes of death.

(2) Obesity is becoming more common among poor people in Africa because of easier access to cheap, high fat, high sugar foods, scientists said last Tuesday.

(3) I think in order to avoid being overweight, we should keep a balanced diet and take regular exercise.

(4) The number of people overweight or obese had increased by nearly 35 percent between the early 1990s and early 2000s.

(5) A 15-year study of nearly 6,000 people shows that being overweight alone is responsible for 11 per cent of cases of heart failure in men and 14 per cent of cases in women.

> **Teaching Notes**
>
> 通过补充完成论点表述,帮助学生学习根据 although/though, but, however 等提示词,用适切、清晰的语言表达观点。可允许不同答案。教师可组织学生展开讨论,并给予语言方面的支持。

Task 4: Complete each thesis statement.

(1) Although cell phones bring great benefits to people, *their negative effects in our daily life cannot be neglected*.

(2) Though many students think that an e-dictionary is undoubtedly better than a paper dictionary, *we can't deny that a paper dictionary has its special charm*.

(3) It is generally believed that being a performer limits a child's formal education, but *some people think that it is necessary for child performers to play roles in some films*.

(4) Some students think that homework is a waste of time. However, *it's believed that homework is a must if students want to consolidate what they have learned and improve their academic performance*.

(5) Many people maintain that children shouldn't be allowed to own or use mobile phones. However, *it's true that mobile phones bring great benefits to children in terms of study*.

(6) Some people argue that single-sex schools are good for education, but *a considerable number of people think that children need to be exposed to the opposite sex in preparation for later life*.

Task 5: Brainstorm examples, facts or statistics to illustrate the effects of online games on students.

> **Teaching Notes**
>
> 本活动旨在通过完成表格指导学生学会使用例子、事实、数据等论证不同观点。教师可以通过"头脑风暴"、小组讨论或者指导学生利用网络资源对目标话题展开讨论。

Effects of Online Games	
Positive effects	**Negative effects**
Playing online games helps reduce pressure, broadens horizons and helps students respond very quickly.	*Playing online games distracts students from study, encourages violence and harms students physically.*
According to the research, games that deal with sports, role-playing and adventure can help students develop different kinds of abilities.	*As some educators put it, children as well as adults playing online games too much tend to isolate themselves and fail to develop relationships with others.*
...	...

Task 6: Write a thesis statement about "effects of online games" and give the evidence.

> **Teaching Notes**
>
> 通过指导学生写出中心论点和论据，使学生掌握常用表达论点的句型和学会选择相关论据。教师可以引导学生基于**Task 5**写出关于网络游戏这一话题的中心论点，表达对网络游戏的态度，然后寻找相关证据论证观点。

Thesis statement: *I firmly believe that online games have negative effects on students.*

Evidence 1: *Apparently playing online games distracts students from study.*

Evidence 2: *Some students who are addicted to online games suffer from some diseases like short-sightedness, headache and obesity.*

Evidence 3: *According to a survey, among those children playing games, 86% do not get enough exercise because they play online games too much.*

3. 构建段落（Develop paragraphs logically）[1]

1）段落内逻辑论证（Develop a logic paragraph）

清晰的段落结构和有效的论证方法是段落生成的两个重要方面。

其中，段落结构分为归纳和演绎；论证方法包括假设、递进、因果、分类、比较、对比等。教师可以指导学生先通过归纳或演绎确立段落内部的基本框架，然后运用多元的逻辑论证方法，确保论述内容与段落观点形成合乎逻辑的关系。

（1）段落结构（The structure of a paragraph）

归纳（inductive reasoning）和演绎（deductive reasoning）是论证的两大基本方法。归纳法在罗列有力论据（如事实、原因、例子、推断等）的基础上，发表观点，得出结论。演绎法则先提出观点，再呈现论据，给出具体翔实的论证。

形象地说，归纳法是一种自下而上的逻辑（bottom-up logic），演绎法是一种自上而下的逻辑（top-down logic）。在写作教学过程中，教师应该指导学生通过归纳或演绎的方法，形成结构完整、逻辑清晰的段落。例如在下文中，作者在第一段运用了归纳法，先论述然后在段落最后一句得出结论；而在第二段运用了演绎法，先提出观点随后展开具体论述。

Sample 1

Should Schools Ask Students to Evaluate Their Teachers?

...

For one thing, students are often too shy or too afraid of confrontation when it comes to assessing their teachers' performance. With little awareness to make their voice heard, they are unlikely to take the initiative to communicate with their teachers face-to-face when they do have some enlightening suggestions. **Therefore, providing an evaluation option gives them a chance to comment on their teachers.**

In addition, **these evaluations give the teachers an opportunity to**

---

[1] 本部分作者为上海市格致中学褚朝慧。

improve their teaching methods and teaching styles. Without feedbacks from their students, teachers might use the same educational technique for years in spite of its ineffectiveness. Because teaching is supposed to be student-centered, students' authentic evaluations are the best reference for teachers. Just like companies base their designs of products on the customers' feedback so that the products can be tailored to their customers, it is the same case with teachers.

...

（2）论证方法（Methods of demonstrating）

段落内的句子之间应该形成紧密的逻辑关系，议论文中的逻辑论证方法通常有假设（assumption）、递进（progression）、因果（cause and effect）、分类（classification）、比较（comparison）、对比（contrast）等。教师可以引导学生有效地运用这些逻辑论证方法，组句成段。

① 假设（Assumption）

假设常由if引出，可分为正面假设和反面假设。假设法为推论的开展铺设条件。无论是正面假设还是反面假设，只要分析到位，都是对段落中心论点的有力论证。例如：

Sample 2

Should Governments Continue to Finance Public Schools?

...

In addition, having sufficient funding makes it possible to hire excellent teachers for public schools. **If governments continue funding public schools, these schools will have sufficient budget to pay for well-qualified teaching staff.** As a famous saying goes, money spent on the brain is never spent in vain. Students benefit a lot from these experienced teachers.

...

> **Sample 3**
>
> ### Is it Important for College Students to Learn Computer Technology?
>
> ...
>
> It is important that college students should learn adequate computer skills. We are living in an Information Age where the Internet is the key to almost all the knowledge and information available. So a good understanding of the computer technology will give a student a favourable competitive edge in our society today. **If one has little knowledge of computer skills, he will probably lag behind the times, being excluded from what is going on in the world.**
>
> ...

在以上两个段落中，作者分别运用了 if 引出正面假设和反面假设。仔细阅读标题和表示假设的句子，可以看出假设对于论证观点的作用。

②递进（Progression）

在段落中，支撑段落论点的通常并不局限于一条理由或一个论据，此时需要用递进关系将各个理由或论据有机整合，增强段落论证的逻辑性。例如：

> **Sample 4**
>
> ### Is Life a Process of Pursuing Excellence?
>
> ...
>
> Life should be spent in active pursuit for something better. **We human beings are by nature a race that is filled with expectation.** This expectation tends to motivate us to make the best of today so as to turn our eagerly anticipated goals into reality as soon as possible. **Besides, it is generally acknowledged that the true meaning of life lies in the sense of feeling self-fulfilled.** If we only took life as it is and did nothing to make it better, most likely we would soon feel at a

loss and be bored to death. **Furthermore, active pursuit for excellence is also of great significance to building up our willpowers and hence developing positive personality.**

...

在以上段落中，如粗体句子所示，作者用表示递进关系的衔接词（besides, furthermore 等）列出了三条理由，层层递进地论证了"人生应该不断地追求更好"的观点。

③ 因果（Cause and effect）

因果论证是一种缜密揭示事物间因果关系的论证方法，在议论文中被广泛运用。使用因果论证时要注意合理推论因果关系，切忌生搬硬套。例如：

Sample 5

...

Watching TV too much tends to have an unfavourable influence on the family relationship. Communication is the key to the harmony of a family. If one spends the vast majority of his spare time on television, the so-called "couch potato" will definitely turn a deaf ear to the emotional need from his family members, which is bound to **result in** the family conflicts, upsetting the family relationship.

...

本段运用了因果论证法。后跟结果的常用词组有 lead to、contribute to、give rise to、bring about、translate into、as a result、as a consequence、result in 等。后跟原因的常用词组有 because of、in that、thanks to、owing to、due to、given、result from、as a result of 等。

④ 分类（Classification）

分类讨论是指从不同角度、不同人群、不同领域等维度分门别类地对论点逐一论证，体现了论证的全面性、综合性和可靠性。例如：

117

Sample 6

...

Different teaching plans allow teachers to employ different teaching methods suited to a particular group. **As for the more intelligent students with a quicker mind and a stronger desire for knowledge**, teachers can involve something more difficult into their lessons, satisfying their extra needs. **As for the students who may be slow at learning or acquiring new knowledge**, a correspondingly suitable teaching strategy then is highly desirable. In this case, giving lessons respectively to students of different levels is generally good for both groups of students, since teachers can design different courses and teaching methods in accordance with their practical needs.

...

作者将学生群体按照学习接受能力的不同分为两类进行探讨分析，最后得出"学生需要教师针对性的分层教学"这一结论。

⑤ 比较（Comparison）

为了论证两者或多者孰优孰劣，需要从不同角度，不同方面进行比较分析。例如：

Sample 7

Is the City Life a Better Choice for Children?

...

Children can enjoy a more colourful life in cities. There are various cultural activities and advanced facilities available for children, such as exhibitions, galleries, museums and theatres. Therefore, children living in cities are **much more** experienced and knowledgeable **than those** in the countryside, who are less culturally educated and informed.

...

作者通过比较城市孩子和农村孩子的文化生活，来支撑其观点"城市孩子的生活更丰富多彩"。比较法常常用于两个观点择其一的议论段落中。

⑥ 对比（Contrast）

使用对比论证时，需要注意对比双方要属于同一范畴，并且对比两方要表现出相反或相对的特点。例如：

Sample 8

Is the Development of Technology Making our Life More Convenient?

...

In the past, when we needed to buy something, we had to go to the shopping mall. **Nowadays**, all can be done with a click and the goods will be delivered home, even at a lower price. And if we want to deposit money into our accounts, we **used to** go directly to a bank and wait for a desperately long queue. **On the contrary**, we may **now** comfortably make full use of the self-banking service at home. Thus, efficiency of work and life has been highly improved owing to the technological advances.

...

本段运用了对比法，对比对象为过去和现在的购物方式和银行业务，以鲜明对比论证了技术进步带来的便捷。

写作实践

Task 1: Write the topic sentence for each paragraph according to the context, and decide whether the development of the paragraph employs deduction or induction.

> **Teaching Notes**
>
> 本活动旨在帮助学生通过仔细观察段落结构和内容，学会写明确的主题句，加深理解并运用归纳及演绎的写作技能。教师需引导学生自主细读段落内的支撑信息，体会主题句与支撑信息间的关系。主题句的答案是开放的。

(A)

We need to set aside some time for physical exercise. When we are facing the stress, we tend to devote ourselves to studying and are too busy to do some exercise. But the truth is that doing sports is an effective way to release stress. I always find myself more productive after jogging or swimming and you should definitely have a try. (*Deductive reasoning*)

(B)

If humans stick to environment friendly concepts and make proper use of natural resources, the environment will undoubtedly serve us well. Nature is always so generous and selfless that it never refuses to provide all the treasures it owns for humans. However, things can be totally the opposite if humans abuse those precious resources. Improper use of natural resources can cause such severe problems as the loss of soil, the expansion of desert and the destruction of ecological environment. Considering the strong connection between humans and the environment, we can draw the conclusion that *we must use natural resources properly*. (*Inductive reasoning*)

(C)

Psychological qualities and morality are of great importance to a student. A full score only proves a student's perfect academic level, but cannot guarantee his or her mental health and sensible behaviour. Psychological qualities enable a person to know how to deal with hardships and difficulties, how to avoid psychological breakdowns, and how to stay positive towards life. Morality, in the meantime, gets people to understand the meaning of responsibility and helps them to distinguish right from wrong. Both of them are necessary parts constituting the health growth of a student into a wise and responsible adult. (*Deductive reasoning*)

Teaching Notes

通过让学生从不同的角度运用不同方法对于同一个观点进行论证的活动，帮助他们操练和运用这些论证的写作技能，为他们打开论证思路。教师可根据学生的学习程度采用不同方法。如：直接给出一组完整的句子，让学生判断运用了何种逻辑论证方法（较易）；或让学生用指定的论证方法（如假设、对比、因果等）构建段落（较难）。答案是开放的，教师可让学生交流讨论，打开思路。

Task 2: Work out your reasoning according to the given viewpoint, using cause and effect, assumption, progression, contrast, classification, etc.

Viewpoint: College students should try

to stand on their own feet and be independent from their parents.

(1) Cause and effect（因果）

Because *the day will finally come when the students have to confront the reality by themselves*, parents cannot pave the way for their children throughout their life. The earlier the little birds fly away, the sooner they can adapt themselves to the changing world.

(2) Assumption（正面假设或反面假设）

Stepping into the university, the students are getting closer to the society. A brand-new life will be presented in front of them. If *they don't make efforts to arrange their own life by themselves*, chances are that *they will also be reluctant to explore the colourful world and shoulder the responsibility in the near future*.

(3) Comparison and contrast（比较与对比）

It is noted that college students in many foreign countries do part-time jobs to make a living and earn their tuition, while many students in China *still rely on their parents both financially and spiritually*. (*contrast*) It turns out that those who become independent at an earlier stage *are more likely to be favoured in the job interviews* than those who are over dependent. (*comparison*)

(4) Progression（递进）

One's college year, especially the junior or the senior, is a stage that bridges the ivory tower and the society. To be well prepared for one's future career, college students should try to stand on their own feet. *What's more/Moreover/Furthermore/In addition/Additionally, sooner or later, they will eventually become parents, which urges them to become mature and shoulder the responsibility for their family*.

(5) Classification（分类）

In terms of college students, *they are destined to support themselves or even care for their parents*. On the part of parents, *they've already been overburdened for so long to raise their kids, so they should let go of them when they go to college*. As for our society, *it always expects its young constructors to take the responsibility and make contributions instead of asking more*.

2）段落间自然衔接（Make smooth transitions between paragraphs）

段与段之间的自然衔接能帮助议论文在论述过程中连贯流畅。衔接方法主要有以下两种。

（1）显性衔接

即在段落间使用连接词或具有衔接功能的词块，使行文结构在形式上清晰明了，具有连贯性。英语重"形合"，强调在语言形式上有鲜明的"路标"。"路标"的作用在于承上启下、标识逻辑关系。写作中的衔接词或衔接短语（transitions）正是"路标"。

（2）隐性衔接

即建立段与段之间逻辑论证的内在联系。值得注意的是，要做到内容上的自然衔接，分论点的主题句至关重要。由于主题句通常出现在段首，段首的表达既要有显性衔接，同时还要切切实实地在内容上合乎段与段之间既定的逻辑关系，切忌不能徒有形式上的衔接。

一篇完整的议论文通常有若干个段落，这些段落均有相对独立的分论点。为了使段落与段落之间连贯流畅，段落衔接词或承上启下的过渡句是必不可少的。例如：

Sample 1

Is it Necessary for Students to Take Extra Courses in Tutorial Centres?

Many parents stick to the opinion that taking courses from tutorial centres enables their children to improve their academic performance. Lots of children have to go for extra lessons regularly, cutting down leisure hours on weekends. But from where I stand, extracurricular tutoring is not a wise choice.

In the first place, most of the tutorial centres are profit-oriented, whose teacher-assessment system is definitely not as qualified as that of the public schools. In many cases, teachers from tutorial centres are part-time workers or even undergraduate students. What's worse, due to the limited class period, they do not know each student well and each individual in the class is given inadequate attention.

Besides, extracurricular tutoring prevents students from learning actively. If one eats too much snacks, he will have no appetite for the main course. It is the same case with off-campus tutoring. Because of the extra help from tutors, students might be less attentive in the class, thus missing important points in class.

Not only do tutorial centres rob students of independent learning, it also lays a heavy burden on the family finance. Some tutorial centres charge parents hundreds of dollars for merely several hours. And at the same time, it takes up too much spare time of the students, which should have been spent with their family members.

In the final analysis, it is undeniable that parents should lay emphasis on children's education, but sometimes they do not give much thought to the effectiveness of extracurricular tutoring. Students are supposed to pay more attention to their study in school rather than depend on tutorial centres.

上文中，作者恰当地运用衔接词或过渡句（如 in the first place、besides、not only ... (but) also ...、in the final analysis），逐个引出分论点及段落。下表列出了常见的衔接词及其作用：

衔接词的作用	衔　接　词
表示顺序	firstly, to begin with, initially, besides, secondly, furthermore, in addition, what's more, last but not least, finally, eventually ...
表示转折	however, but, meanwhile, in spite of the fact that ...
引出结论	to sum up, in summary, from what has been mentioned, in short, to conclude, on the whole, all in all ...

写作实践

Task 1: Read the following passage and pick out the transitional phrases (or sentences) and figure out their functions.

> **Teaching Notes**
>
> 本活动旨在帮助学生通过圈划衔接词或衔接句，增强使用衔接词或句的意识，并明确每一类衔接词或句的作用。

Should University Students Do an Internship?

Faced with the fierce competition in the job market, a majority of university students choose to do internships in response to the increasingly high demands. As far as I am concerned, doing an internship prepares college students for their future career as long as they do it in a sensible way.

To begin with , an internship offers a golden chance for students to put knowledge into practice. In spite of all of the years spent in the university preparing to enter the workplace, many graduates say that they struggle with the shift from classroom to career world and find book knowledge of little use when it comes to practical situations. In this case, if they have some intern experience beforehand, they will be familiar with the realities of the workplace.

Transitional phrases（表示层层推进，引出结论）

In addition , to perform well in the workplace, students are required to be a good teamwork player, which can only be trained in the real working environment. It is essential to know how to interact with co-workers and to participate collectively in teamwork. Since conducting one's study is relatively personal, students need internships to make up for the important lesson of team working.

Although overwhelming advantages of internships are presented, internships still have a negative effect on college students if not properly dealt with. For example, a full schedule for working will distract a student from his study, putting the cart before the horse. It is a waste of time for an education major to take part-time job as a model because it's irrelevant to his future career.

Transitional sentence（表示转折）

To sum up , college education, combined with relevant working experience, is a better way of cultivating a promising graduate. Internships done in moderation will be a positive experience in one's future career.

Task 2: Rearrange the following paragraphs.

Teaching Notes

本活动旨在帮助学生通过给段落重新排序来理解议论文段落之间的逻辑关系。

The Importance of Being a Good Listener

Nowadays, we live in a world where there are more social networks but less effective communication. People tend to simply define communication as talking and expressing while the fact is that listening plays an essential role in communication.

① In the final place, when someone is telling you something about his suffering, he may not be expecting you to solve the problems, instead, he is expressing himself in an attempt to be understood, which will make him feel relieved. You just need to prepare your ears and be a considerate listener.

② First and foremost, only when you listen carefully can you make sure that you have figured out what the speaker really wants. Otherwise, you might miss some important points. Even worse, listening carelessly could mislead you to do something wrong.

③ Conclusion can be drawn safely that listening is the key to effective communication. Listening serves as a bridge that connects people.

④ In addition, a good listener makes people feel respected, which is the precondition of good communication. If you listen to someone carefully with frequent eye contact and active response, the speaker will be glad to know that you are taking his words seriously, and they feel safe to open up their heart.

②→④→①→③

Task 3: Fill in the blanks with proper transitions according to the logic of each paragraph.

Teaching Notes

本活动旨在增强学生段落衔接意识,强化学生在段首运用恰当的段落衔接词的能力,并将此能力迁移至学生的习作中。允许多种答案,可让学生充分讨论交流,加深理解。

The Best Way to Stay Healthy

It is true that nowadays people are becoming increasingly aware of the importance of health. I hold the golden rule that the best way to stay fit is to combine moderate physical exercise with a balanced diet. The reasons can be listed as follows.

(1) *For one thing/On one hand/In the first place/Firstly/First and foremost/ To begin with*, physical exercise can do good to our body, including losing fat, strengthening the immune system and lowering the risk of heart attack. What's more, smooth emotion and good mood are actually closely related to physical health.

(2) *For another/On the other hand/Besides/Moreover/Furthermore*, a balanced diet can provide a person with the right kind and amount of nutrition required for body functioning. Since the body needs various nutrients, we should balance our food intake to guarantee an adequate supply of nutrients.

(3) *To sum up/In summary/Above all/To conclude/In short/On the whole/All in all*, only by taking a balanced diet and doing moderate physical exercise can we keep fit.

第六章 应用文写作（**Practical Writing**）[①]

一、应用文的定义和分类（Definition and Classification of Practical Writing）

1. 应用文的定义（Definition of Practical Writing）

Definition of Practical Writing

Practical writing communicates specific and factual information to a particular audience for a specific purpose. It is only part of non-literature written English. It generally refers to as those common written documents for special purposes and in regular forms. The information is practical in nature, and this is what makes practical writing different from other types of writing.

应用文是人们在生活、学习、工作中为处理实际事务而进行的写作。应用文通常有特定的读者，并有惯用格式。应用文写作是为了公务或个人事务而写，用于解决实际问题的，被广泛地运用于日常生活中，具有其特别的实用意义。

2. 应用文的分类（Classification of Practical Writing）

英语应用文种类繁多。针对高中英语教学的实际情况，本章介绍日常生活与学习中经常使用的几种应用文，包括信件、日记、通知、新闻、个人陈述、广告及海报等。在内容编排上也根据学生对各类文体掌握程度的不同而有所侧重。

二、应用文写作的要点（Essentials of Practical Writing）

Essentials of Practical Writing

1. Write with a specific purpose

[①] 本章作者为上海市晋元高级中学汤晓华、华东师范大学第二附属中学黄雷、上海市黄浦区教育学院金敏、上海市新中高级中学王慧敏、上海市长宁区教育学院陈德江、上海大学附属中学肖丹、上海市奉贤中学蔡东慧。

2. Use appropriate language

3. Write in a fixed layout

1. 写作目的明确(Write with a specific purpose)

应用文不是供人审美或欣赏的文体，而是在生活、学习中运用，起到一定功能，达到一定目的的文体。应用文是为实现特定目的服务的，如告知、道歉、邀请、陈述等，其写作动因与目的十分明确。

2. 语言表达得体(Use appropriate language)

应用文的文本形式有特定要求，讲究规范。在实际写作中，不同种类的应用文对于语言表达都有特定的要求，应根据不同的读者和内容使用相应的语言。

3. 格式体例规范(Write in a fixed layout)

应用文有固定的通用格式和体例，体现了该文体的规范性和严肃性，在应用文写作时必须遵守格式体例的要求。譬如英语信件通常由信头、日期、称呼、信件主体、结尾敬语、署名等构成；日记的格式通常包括书端（注明日期、天气等）和正文；个人陈述的格式和通知的格式也是完全不同的。

三、应用文写作的常用写作技巧（Basic Skills in Practical Writing）

Basic Skills in Practical Writing

1. Identify the reader

2. Formalize the layout

3. Choose the language

明确应用文的读者、采用规范的格式和选择得体恰当的语体是应用文写作的常用技巧。不同种类应用文的技巧有细微的差别。

1. 确定读者(Identify the reader)

应用文是反映客观事物、将特定信息或内容传递给某一特定读者（群）的书面语言，它的功能为完成具体工作或作为办事的工具。在写作前要注意分析读者，明确读者是谁，再根据读者，进一步确定该使用什么语体。

写作实践

Task 1: Read the following samples and fill in the table with the information you've got.

Sample 1

June 8th, 2011

Dear Sir or Madam,

　　My name is Li Ming, a student from Mingqi Middle School. It is said that there is a poverty-relief programme launched by the World Child Foundation. I'm writing to apply for a fund of 2,000 yuan to carry out my project to help the children in poverty-stricken areas.

　　Firstly, I will spend 500 yuan on pens and notebooks they need. Secondly, I will buy some tools to help them repair their school buildings, desks and chairs. This will cost me 1,000 yuan. Lastly, I will invite a psychologist to give the left-over children a lesson because without their parents around them, they must feel very lonely, and it will cost 500 yuan.

　　I really want to try my best to help them. The fund will help me realize my dream. My e-mail is 2011hope@hotmail.com. I'm looking forward to your reply.

Yours sincerely,

Li Ming

Sample 2

NOTICE

　　The visit to Shanghai Natural History Museum originally scheduled for Wednesday, March 9, is now put off till next Friday, March 18. Please assemble at the school gate at 1 : 00 p.m.

The Students' Union

March 6, 2016

Sample 3

Dear Anne,

  Thank you for your invitation to dinner at your home tomorrow evening. Unfortunately, it is much to my regret that I cannot join you and your family, because I will be fully occupied then for an important exam coming the day after tomorrow. I feel terribly sorry for missing the chance of such a happy get-together, and I hope that all of you have a good time. Is it possible for you and me to have a private meeting afterward? If so, please don't hesitate to drop me a line about your preferable date. I do long for a pleasant chat with you.

  Please allow me to say sorry again.

Regards,

Li Ming

Sample 4

Résumé

  First Name: Mandy

  Last Name: Snyder

  Address: 6 Oak Street, Arlington, VA 12333

  Phone: 555—555—1234

  Email: mandysnyder@gmail.com

  Education: Arlington High School, Arlington, Virginia 2012—Present

        GPA: 3.81

Achievements:

- National Honor Society: 2012, 2013, 2014
- Academic Honor Roll: 2014—2015

Work Experience:

Sales Associate, The Retail Store

June 2013—Present

- Maintain and restock inventory
- Provide customer service
- Responsible for training incoming associates in operating cash register system due to track record of excellence

Child Care: 2010—Present

- Provide childcare for half a dozen families after school, weekends, and during school vacations
- Develop and implement fun and educational activities for all children, ranging from ages 1 year to 8 years

Volunteer Experience: Arlington Literacy Program

- Run book monthly for six eight-year-olds

Run for Life:

- Assist in marketing (via social media), setting up booths, running registration, and cleaning up for bi-annual race

Interests/Activities:

- Member of Arlington High School Tennis Team
- Girl Scout
- Piano, 10 years

Sample	Target Reader	Purpose	Language (formal/informal)
1	*persons in charge of World Child Foundation*	*to apply for the fund*	*formal*
2	*students who are going to visit the museum*	*to inform of the change*	*formal*

(Continued on the next page)

Sample	Target Reader	Purpose	Language (formal/informal)
3	*Anne, a friend to host a dinner party*	*to apologize for not being able to attend the party*	*informal*
4	*persons in charge of student admission or enrollment*	*to apply for the admission to university*	*formal*

2. 规范格式（Formalize the layout）

1）信件的规范格式

英语书信针对某一特定目的（感谢、投诉、道歉、邀请、申请等），写给特定的读者，有其特定的格式和结构，通常由信头、称呼、信件主体、结尾敬语及署名等部分构成。

阅读以下信件并仔细观察它的格式与结构。

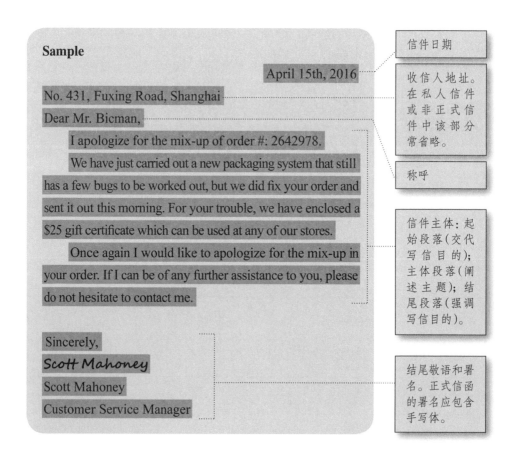

Sample

April 15th, 2016

No. 431, Fuxing Road, Shanghai

Dear Mr. Bicman,

I apologize for the mix-up of order #: 2642978.

We have just carried out a new packaging system that still has a few bugs to be worked out, but we did fix your order and sent it out this morning. For your trouble, we have enclosed a $25 gift certificate which can be used at any of our stores.

Once again I would like to apologize for the mix-up in your order. If I can be of any further assistance to you, please do not hesitate to contact me.

Sincerely,

Scott Mahoney

Scott Mahoney

Customer Service Manager

信件日期

收信人地址。在私人信件或非正式信件中该部分常省略。

称呼

信件主体：起始段落（交代写信目的）；主体段落（阐述主题）；结尾段落（强调写信目的）。

结尾敬语和署名。正式信函的署名应包含手写体。

一般来说，信件包括以下一些内容：

（1）信头（Heading）

包括日期和收信人地址。书信日期可用各种方式书写，如15(th) April 2016，或April 15(th)，2016，又或15/04/2016等。在商务信函中应规范书写日期，不宜采用省略形式。在商务信函中，如不是专用信笺，一般需写上完整的地址，但如果是私人信函的话，地址可以省略。

（2）称呼（Salutation）

根据与收信人熟悉程度，采用不同的书信称呼，以下可供参考：

Dear+Mr/Mrs/Ms/Miss+Surname,（当作者明确了解收信人的姓名或性别时使用此类称呼）；

Dear Sir or Madam, (or Dear Sir/Madam,) To whom it may concern,（当作者并不了解收信人的姓名或性别时可使用此类称谓）。

（3）信件主体（Body of the letter）

英语信函通常由三部分构成：起始段落、主体段落、总结段落。起始段落往往直接交代写信目的；主体段落通常应该清晰、全面、有逻辑地阐述主题；结尾段落可再次强调写信目的。如果是申请信、投诉信等，还应写清联系方式，便于对方答复。

（4）结尾敬语（Complimentary closing）

视与收信人的关系亲密程度，以下结尾敬语可供参考：

Yours faithfully, Yours sincerely,（当不了解收信人姓名或正式信函可采用）；

Yours,（与收信人关系友好，但并不亲密时使用）；

Love/Lots of love,（与收信人关系亲密，感情深厚时使用）。

写作实践

Teaching Notes

通过信件阅读及完成相关练习，帮助学生了解信件的框架结构。

Task 1: Read the letter to find out the function of each part and write them in the box.

4 December 2015

Dear Manager,　　(1) *salutation*

I write this letter to place a complaint against the bad delivery service of your company. ·········· (2) *purpose (to complain)*

The Apple iPad I ordered from your company arrived yesterday. I am sorry to find that the packing case was broken and that the home button of the device was struck and could not work. What's more, there were some scratches on the surface of the tablet. Since there is such damage to the goods, I decide to file a complaint against the delivery service. ·········· (3) *details of the problem*

Would you let me know whether I should return the iPad for a replacement or if I can get refunded? I will hold on to this iPad until I hear from you. I would like to have this matter settled by 18 December, or I will appeal to the press. ·········· (4) *appeal*

Yours sincerely,

Pool George ·········· (5) *complimentary closing and signature*

Task 2: Read the following parts carefully and put them in the right order. ··········

> **Teaching Notes**
> 通过让学生组织信件内容，使他们加深对信件结构和内容安排的理解。

(1) Therefore, I do hope to exchange it for another camera or declare a refund. I would appreciate it if my problem could receive due attention.

(2) I am writing to bring your attention to the quality of the digital camera (NIKON 453) I bought last Friday at your store.

(3) During the five days the camera has been in my possession, problems have emerged one after another. For one thing, the screen is always black, making the camera no different from a traditional one. For another, the battery is distressing as it supports the operation for only two hours.

2 April 2016

Dear Sir,

a. *(2)* _____

b. *(3)* _____

c. *(1)* _____

Yours faithfully,

Chen Ying

Task 3: Fill in the blanks and make the following application letter complete.

Teaching Notes

本活动帮助学生通过完成信件具体了解并体会信件各部分的功能和内容。填空(2)、(4)的答案因人而异，但是填空(2)必须包括联系方式和时间，以及结束的礼貌用语。

(1) *Dear Sir or Madam,*

My name is Li Hua. I'd like to apply for the job as a waitress at your restaurant which was advertised in Saturday's *China Daily*.

I have worked as a waitress for about 3 months at the Olympic Diner. Since both my parents often speak English at home, I can basically speak English as fluently as I speak Chinese. I'm interested in a part-time position.

(2) *Please contact me at the following address or e-mail: bertha@yahoo.com or call me at 1376147324. You can get hold of me any time before noon. Thank you for considering my application and I am looking forward to your early reply.*

(3) *Yours faithfully,*

(4) *Li Hua*

2）日记的规范格式

书端和正文是英文日记的两个重要组成部分。

书端是指正文前面的星期、日期、天气。星期和日期位于左上角，右上角写当天的天气状况。比如，drizzle（毛毛雨）、overcast（阴）、fine（晴）、thundering（雷雨）、shower（阵雨）、icy cold（寒冷），等等。天气状况并不是必写的项目。

日记正文有时可根据作者需要写上日记的小标题以突出中心内容（如Sample 1）。但因日记是作者在日常生活中对于发生的事情和自己感受与情感的记录，通常不加标题。

正文为日记的主体，主要内容来源于生活，可长可短。叙事、描述、说明、抒情、议论都可以。日记内容常为叙事，因此时态多为过去时，但也因内容不同而灵活使用。例如：

Sample 1

Sun., 26 June 2016   Fine

Attitude is Everything

I had a friend named Li Yi. He was the kind of guy who was always in a good mood and always had something positive to say. He was a top student in our class, ...

Sample 2

Saturday, January 16   Snowy

Today I went to the market to buy some tomatoes.

When I got there, I found that I had left my wallet at home. Oh, no!

...

3）通知的规范格式

通知是短小的正规文体。一份通知的字数一般为40—50个词，但必须包括如下信息：事件、地点、时间、参加对象。例如：

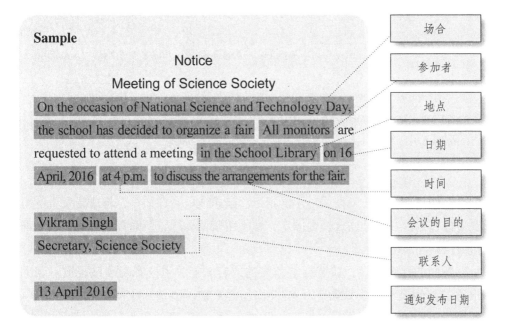

 写作实践

Task 4: Read the notice and find out the event, time, attendants, and contact person.

Teaching Notes

　　本活动旨在帮助学生了解和掌握通知的格式、内容等。

Notice

Sandhya Tara

Our school is organizing a cultural programme to collect funds for "Sandhya Tara", a home for the elderly. We plan to include a dance drama, a magic show and other items. Students who wish to participate should submit their names before 20 June, 2016.

Sandeep Walia

Secretary, Cultural Society

10 June 2016

Item	Details
Occasion	*a cultural programme to collect funds for "Sandyhya Tara", a home for the elderly*
Attendant	*students who wish to participate in the dance drama, the magic show, etc.*
Date	*before 20 June, 2016*
Contact person	*Sandeep Walia, secretary of Cultural Society*

4）新闻的一般格式

新闻写作常用于学校或单位的报纸、杂志或电台广播稿，将最新发生的重要事件告知读者。其格式较为固定，通常由新闻标题、新闻首句或首段、新闻过渡及新闻结尾组成。

新闻的标题简短，应能反映新闻的内容又能吸引读者阅读该报道。新闻报道的首句最重要，通常句子较长，包含人物、事件、时间和地点等要素。新闻报道的第一段通常包括所有的重要信息，而后面的段落是对首段的补充。例如：

Sample

English Spelling Contest Closed Last Week

In order to help teenagers enlarge vocabulary and cultivate their love for English, a spelling contest was held in Mingqi Middle School last Sunday, December 11th, 2015. 200 senior students from grade one and two gathered in the gymnasium together, spelling words from easy to difficult and having pair-work competition.

Li Ming won the first prize with the scores of 80 words per minute. He also broke our school record that had been kept for nearly 2 years. The genius following the champion was Zhang Hua. With her good memory, she spelt 73 words without a mistake. We have also seen some satisfying things in the contest. For example, students have improved a lot in their oral pronunciation this time, as well as their handwriting.

A good command of English is essential in today's life, especially in an international city like Shanghai. More students should be involved in such activities, and if you try this, I promise that you will find great interest in it!

写作实践

Task 5: Decide the correct order of the following parts of a news story.

> **Teaching Notes**
> 本活动旨在帮助学生了解和掌握新闻报道的基本结构。

A. Superintendent Putman first proposed this plan in November, but the district did not have the funding to go forward.

B. "Giving free Wi-Fi to our students will enable them to do research, read the news or even watch educational videos each day," Superintendent Kelli Putman said. "This change will have a positive impact on academic productivity."

C. Students who ride the school bus to and from school will have access to the Internet during their commute starting from March 1.

D. "With the tight budget and tough economic times, I thought my Wi-Fi proposal was a pipe dream," she said. "I want to thank the donor for being so generous."

E. The city newspaper published an article about the proposal, and the anonymous donation followed.

$C \rightarrow B \rightarrow A \rightarrow E \rightarrow D$

5）个人陈述的规范格式

个人陈述常用于求职应聘或申请入学，通常分为开头、正文和结尾三部分。开头部分讲明申请的目的；正文部分突出个人经历，选用最能体现自己特点的事例来说明自己就是最符合招生或招聘单位要求的人，帮助他们对自己进行全面深入的了解；结尾部分重申自己渴求就读于该校或就职于该机构的强烈愿望，以达到被录取或录用的目的。

3. 选择语言（Choose the language）

因读者的不同，应用文要选择不同的语言。如个人陈述、道歉信、投诉信等应采用较为正式的语体，语言要规范、准确；日记、广告等的语言则比较轻松、活泼。

1）信件写作中的语言选择

投诉信是较为正式的书信形式。投诉原因的表述要直接、清晰；叙事应客观、准确、简洁、有逻辑；提出的解决方案要合理、可行；运用的语言宜正式、恰当。

Sample

June 3, 2016

Dear Sir,

I am writing to you about a most unhappy experience.

Last Tuesday, we took a bus of your company from the People's Square to Wuxi. The bus started at 8 a.m., and was scheduled to arrive at 12 at noon. But it stopped midway for mechanical problems. The driver could neither solve the problem nor seek help from others. We had no choice but to stay on the bus for nearly 7 hours. Up until 3 p.m., another bus came to pick us up to Wuxi. We wasted a lot of time and no one explained anything to us or apologized for that.

I suggest that you look into the matter immediately and deal with it quickly and properly.

I am looking forward to your reply.

Sincerely yours,

Zhang Hua

写作实践

Task 1: Match these informal expressions with their formal equivalents.

> **Teaching Notes**
>
> 本活动帮助学生体会正式与非正式的语言表达。

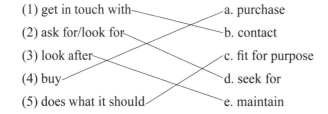

(1) get in touch with — a. purchase
(2) ask for/look for — b. contact
(3) look after — c. fit for purpose
(4) buy — d. seek for
(5) does what it should — e. maintain

2）通知写作中的语言选择

通知中所传达的信息内容必须清晰，不能引起误解或者疑惑。可以使用标准的缩写。此外，为了使通知能迅速引起读者的注意，可以使用粗体字、吸引眼球的标语和令人印象深刻的表达。

Sample

Notice

Found—A Sports Bag

A sports bag was found on the playground on 9 May, 2016 during the break period. Anyone who has misplaced a grey sports bag with huge pockets can collect it from the undersigned within two days, that is, by 12 May, 2016.

John Mattew

(Head Boy)

10 May 2016

> 粗体字,简洁的标题吸引读者注意。

> 画线部分提供关键信息,语言清晰简洁。

📚 **写作实践**

Task 2: Read the following notice and tell what information you can get and how it is stated.

> **Teaching Notes**
>
> 本活动帮助学生具体了解和感悟通知写作的特点和要点。

Appeal

33rd Blood Donation Camp on Sunday 19th August, 2016

Place: Lake Club

Time: 9 : 00 A.M. to 5 : 30 P.M.

All citizens are requested to donate blood for noble cause. Your blood is precious and every drop is a source of life for another.

If you don't know your blood type, we provide free service for determining the blood group.

Refreshments like Protein Drink and others will also be provided to the donors. You will also be facilitated with a Trophy.

Organized by Hajasu Charitable Trust, Pattaya.

Contact:
Office—901-22783389
Mobile—901-338922747

（1）关于此次活动的关键信息和相关事宜，如活动时间与地点、活动组织者、活动目的和意义、联系方式等。

（2）标题Appeal用粗体，以吸引读者注意；用清晰简洁的语言告知关键信息。

3）新闻写作中的语言选择

新闻写作的语言应简洁、客观。语言的简洁指新闻开头直接指向新闻的五要素：人物、事件、时间、地点和原因。譬如报道德国学生到访学校，开头需要阐明多少德国学生，什么时间到访，访问多长时间，以及访问的安排和目的等。语言的客观指新闻写作无需加入作者的观点和态度。

Sample

Mingqi High School received a group of 28 students from Germany last week. During their one-week stay in Shanghai, the students experienced the campus life of Chinese students. They also visited some places of interest in Shanghai and learned about the local culture. The German students were impressed by the kindness of Chinese students, cleanness of the city and taste of the food. In return, 28 students were invited to visit Germany next March.

写作实践

Task 3: Write a news report about the school sports meeting held.

Teaching Notes

让学生通过具体实践，掌握新闻写作的要点，如语言简洁客观，新闻要素必须交代清楚等。

The 25th School Sports Meeting was held on October 14. 350 students from 40 classes entered for 26 sports events. The athletes broke 15 school records and displayed high spirits.

4）个人陈述写作中的语言选择

在撰写个人陈述时，申请人可结合个人的学习和生活经历，挑选典型的事例进行阐述，着重提及自己的思考和收获，使用关键词来突出自己的优势。例如：一位一直关注残疾人生活境遇的学生，想申请政治学和社会服务专业，重点研究残疾人福利政策。他的个人陈述中有这样一段：

I am passionate about the well-beings of the disabled in our society. Having had a very precious opportunity to take part in an exchange programme, I wrote a research report on how the challenged were treated in different countries. I organized a club, doing some research on caring for the disabled. We visited schools for the disabled to do voluntary work, and then I sent a letter to the mayor, giving suggestions on this issue. I hope to study political science and social services focusing on social welfare policies.

在以上段落里申请人选用了非常重要的材料来支持其申请。通过运用生动具体的形容词（短语），动词（短语）及名词（短语），如passionate about, wrote a research report, doing some research on caring for the disabled等强有力地说明了申请人对残疾人的关注和其专业兴趣，向招生官证明申请人是一个充满正能量、关爱他人、有志于研究社会福利政策的人。

5）广告及海报写作中的语言选择

广告或海报的目的就是广而告之，把信息传递给读者，有效地吸引读者、并说服他们接受你的宣传或产品。广告或海报的语言简单、生动、形象、富有感情色彩和感染力。例如：

Sample

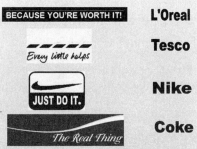

📚 写作实践

Task 4: Write an advertisement to sell a house.

As an agent in a real estate agency, you'd like to write an advertisement to sell the house below.

> **Teaching Notes**
>
> 通过此活动,可以让学生动笔尝试,体会广告或海报中语言的要求,如使用能吸引人的形容词或动词,又如语言简洁精炼等。教师可提供相应词库便于学生区分遴选,同时鼓励学生运用想象力。

Words for reference

---

modern, detached, spacious, well stocked garden, new roof, attractive, wide patio doors, delightful, elegant oak staircase, clean, bright, light ...

Comfortable family home with large garden on north side of town.

Three bedrooms, living room, kitchen, bathroom.

A good price offered.

Modern, spacious house features cozy living room with wood burning fireplace, hardwood flooring, updated, beautiful eat-in kitchen with granite counter tops, newer stainless appliances, private dining room with walkout patio leading off to double-sized backyard with above ground pool. Three spacious bedrooms, sundeck off of second level bedroom. Fantastic family oriented neighbourhood.

Contact John Smith on 6711930 for further information.

第七章　写作教学实践

一、描述性写作教学实践①（Practice on Descriptive Writing）

Writing Task　Write a descriptive paragraph to introduce your favourite place. ②

此写作任务的重点是通过细腻生动的描写，介绍一个自己喜欢的地方。

> **Teaching Focus**
> ◇ Create a dominant impression
> ◇ Use sensory words
> ◇ Choose the order of location

> **Teaching Notes**
> 通过问题引导学生发现、思考和理解范文作者的写作意图和技巧。
> 指导学生阅读范文时，要重点关注其写作目的，作者希望传递给读者一种怎样的感觉，以及作者是怎样根据写作目的选取和组织细节的。

Prewriting

Step 1　Read the sample paragraph.

Read the paragraph below and answer the questions.

> Every time I walk into my apartment, I feel an immediate sense of warmth. The front door opens into our living room, which is usually untidy as this is the place where we relax, watch TV or listen to music. As you go inside, you can see doors leading to three bedrooms and two bathrooms. My bedroom is the smallest one. It has a single bed and a dressing table next to the window. Next to my bedroom there is a bright kitchen with a

---

① 各类文体写作教学实践提供学生使用的任务单，请登录"世纪外语网"（www.century-english.com），进入"下载中心"，搜索关键词"高中英语写作教学"获取配套教学资源包。

② 本案例作者为上海市徐汇区教育学院孟莎。

large wooden table, where we all sit chatting merrily on evenings. The air is usually fi with the delicious smells of my mother's cooking. When my friends come to visit, they describe it as a dream apartment, but to me it is just "home, sweet home".

Questions

(1) What dominant impression does the writer convey in the paragraph?

Warm and sweet.

(2) What sensory details are used in this paragraph?

Sense of warmth, a bright kitchen, a large wooden table, the delicious smells of my mother's cooking.

(3) How does the writer organize the details?

The writer uses signal words of location to organize the details, for example, the front door opens into our living room ..., As you go inside ..., Next to my bedroom ...

Step 2　Choose a topic.

1. Complete the topic chart. List two or three places you think will be interesting to talk about for each category.

> **Teaching Notes**
>
> 通过本活动,引导学生从home, school 以及 other places 三个方面开展"头脑风暴",开阔思路,选择话题。
>
> 在活动中,教师要引导学生关注所选话题是否合适(不宜过大或过小,能吸引读者,能够驾驭)。教师还可以一个话题做示范,提醒学生在写作过程中应该注意的问题。

Example

Places	Specific Topics	
Home	• *my bedroom* • *the living room*	• *the kitchen* • *the garden*
School	• *the classroom* • *the school snack bar*	• *the library* • *the gym*
Other places	• *the underground station* • *the city museum*	• *the bookstore* • *the restaurant*

147

2. Discuss the following questions with your partners.

- Is any of the topics too broad?
- Which topic would the readers enjoy most?
- What sensory details can we use to describe this place?

3. Write down the topic you have chosen and the reason why you choose it.

Example

My topic is *the school snack bar* because *it is the place I always go to during breaks*.

Step 3　Determine the writing purpose and collect details.

1. Think about the feelings or mood you want to convey in the paragraph.

Example

small but warm, homely, comfortable ...

2. Gather sensory details for your description by completing the sensory chart.

Example

Topic	I see ...	I smell ...	I hear ...	I taste ...	I touch/feel ...
the school snack bar	*a spotless counter* *a shiny table* *the menu* *bread* *giant pictures* *the cash register*	*freshly made coffee* *a sweet scent of cream*	*light music* *loud talk*	*coffee*	*hungry* *warm*

3. Cross out the ones that do not serve your purpose.

Example

Topic	I see ...	I smell ...	I hear ...	I taste ...	I touch/feel ...
the school snack bar	*a spotless counter* *a shiny table* *the menu* *bread* *giant pictures* ~~*the cash register*~~	*freshly made coffee* *a sweet scent of cream*	*light music* ~~*loud talk*~~	~~*coffee*~~	*hungry* *warm*

Step 4   Organize details.

Decide which order works best for your description. Then write an organizing list.

> **Teaching Notes**
>
> 本活动在前一活动的基础上，帮助学生选择和确定空间描写顺序，并有序地组织相关的感官细节，让描写更有条理。

Example

Organizing List

	Location verbs/Prepositional phrases	Sensory details
(1)	*walk into the ...*	*pleasant smell of coffee, a counter*
(2)	*on the left side of the counter*	*a coffee machine*

(Continued on the next page)

	Location verbs/Prepositional phrases	Sensory details
(3)	*on the right*	*freshly baked bread and cakes*
(4)	*above the counter*	*giant pictures*
(5)	*...*	*...*

Drafting and Revising

Step 5 Write a topic sentence.

Write a topic sentence and share it with your peers. Use the checklist below to help you.

Checklist

☐ Is the topic sentence clearly stated?

☐ Does the topic sentence have a clear focus?

Teaching Notes

本活动旨在引导学生确定语段主题。如有必要，教师可适当讲解示范，帮助学生了解怎样写主题句。值得注意的是，并不是所有的描述性段落都有一个主题句，但通常开头都有一句话点明主题。

Example

My topic sentence: *My favourite place is the school snack bar, which is small but quite comfortable*.

Step 6 Complete your first draft.

Complete the paragraph organizer and then write a paragraph according to it. When drafting, bear the following questions in mind.

Teaching Notes

使用 Descriptive Paragraph Organizer 来完成初稿可以帮助学生更好地把握文章的整体结构和布局，同时在学生自评和互评时能更方便、更清楚地看出存在的问题。

- What dominant impression do I want to convey in my description?
- What sensory details do I need to use?
- Do they work together to convey this dominant impression?
- Are there any details unrelated?

Descriptive Paragraph Organizer

Example

Topic: *The School Snack Bar*

Topic sentence:

My favourite place is the school snack bar, which is small but quite comfortable.

Detail 1:

You find yourself surrounded by the pleasant smell of coffee.

Detail 2:

On the left side of the counter, there is a coffee machine which may produce superb tasting coffee and hot beverages.

Detail 3:

On the right, there is freshly baked bread and cakes.

Detail 4:

Right above the counter are giant pictures of sandwiches and salads. I like salads because I believe vegetables are good for our health.

Detail 5:

Susan, the hostess is wiping the counter as usual. "Hey, you," she says.

Closing:

As you sit down, all the tiredness is gone, and the only thing left in your mind is to enjoy this relaxing moment.

The first draft[1]

The School Snack Bar

My favourite place is the school snack bar, which is small but quite

---

[1] 由于初稿和修改稿均为写作中的过程稿，所以本章的 "The first draft" 和 "The improved version" 保留了撰写过程中存在的语言错误。

comfortable. The minute you walk into it, you will find yourself surrounded by the pleasant smell of coffee. The counter is right before you. On the left side of the counter, there is a coffee machine which may produce superb tasting coffee and hot beverages. On the right, there is freshly baked bread and cakes. Right above the counter are giant pictures of sandwiches and salads. I like salads because I believe vegetables are good for our health. Susan, the hostess is wiping the counter as usual. "Hey, you," she says. As you sit down, all the tiredness is gone, and the only thing left in your mind is to enjoy this relaxing moment.

Step 7   Self-check and peer check.

Revise your first draft using the questions below as a guide.

Teaching Notes

通过检查列表，为学生审视和改进自己的初稿提供思考的方向，并帮助他们依据这些问题对同伴的作品提出修改意见。注意在学生互评时，检查列表的人称要作相应变化。

在起始阶段，教师还应该通过对样本的分析，帮助学生学会如何进行自我修正和同伴互助。教师可根据具体的写作要求，从结构、内容和语言等方面设计适合自己课堂和学生的评价工具。

Checklist

☐ Have I included enough sensory details about the place?

☐ Do I use the proper order of location to organize the details?

☐ Does it sound like I really care about the place?

☐ Do I use descriptive words?

☐ Do my sentences flow smoothly?

☐ Do I use varied sentence patterns?

The improved version

My favourite place is the school snack bar, which is small but quite comfortable. The minute you walk into it, you will find yourself surrounded by the pleasant smell of coffee *mixed with the sweet scent of cream* ① . The counter is right before you. On the left side of the counter, there is a coffee machine which may produce superb tasting fresh coffee and hot beverages. On the right, there is freshly baked bread and cakes. Right above the counter, *giant pictures of sandwiches and salads are hung on the wall* ② . ~~I like salads because I believe vegetables are good for our health.~~ ③ Susan, the hostess is wiping the counter as usual *even though it's spotless* ④ . "Hey, you," she says. *She greets all her regular customers this way.* ⑤ As you sit down, all the tiredness is gone, and the only thing left in your mind is to enjoy this relaxing moment.

修改说明：
① 使用感官细节（嗅觉）。
② 变换句子结构。
③ 删除不相关的细节。
④ 使用感官细节（视觉）。
⑤ 使句子过渡更流畅。

Editing and Proofreading

Step 8　Once you have completed your revising, improve the language of your essay and make sure that there are no mistakes in punctuation, capitalization, spelling and grammar. Then write a neat final copy to share.

Teaching Notes

本环节旨在帮助学生进一步审读自己的作品，确保语法、拼写、标点等准确无误并润色语言。

Model essay

My favourite place is the school snack bar, which is small but quite comfortable. The minute you walk in, you find yourself surrounded by the delicious smell of coffee mixed with the sweet scent of cream. The counter is straight ahead of you. On the left- hand-side is a coffee machine which makes the best-tasting fresh coffee and hot drinks. To the right is a range of freshly baked bread and cakes. On the wall above the counter, there are giant pictures of sandwiches and salads. Susan, the waitress, is wiping the counter, as usual, even though it's spotless. "Hey, you," she says. She greets all her regular customers that way. As soon as you sit down, all your tiredness disappears and all you want to do is relax and enjoy the moment.

二、记叙文写作教学实践（Practice on Narrative Writing）

Writing Task   Write a story on the theme "friendship".[①]

Teaching Focus

◇ Use suspense to arouse readers' interest

◇ Use contrast to highlight the uniqueness of the main character

Prewriting

Teaching Notes

通过阅读范文及回答相关问题，引导学生在记叙文的写作中关注设置悬念和对比描写这两种写作手法。

Step 1   Read the sample passage.

1. Read the story and answer the questions.

There was a time when Whitney didn't have a lot of friends. She was a bit shy and reserved. She never really wanted to be popular, but she did want to have someone to share secrets and laughs with. All through high school, though, she just slipped in and out of "light" friendships where she didn't find a lot of comfort or companionship.

When it came time to go to college, Whitney was quite nervous. She was going to be rooming with someone she didn't know and living in a town 300 miles away from home. There wouldn't be a single person she knew in town. She had no idea how she was going to make friends in this new environment.

---

① 本案例作者为华东师范大学第一附属中学姜振骅。

The first week of classes, one thing changed Whitney's life forever. In her English Composition class, she was asked to share a little about herself. She told everyone where she called home and all of the other ordinary details that students share in such situations. The final question for each student was always the same: "What is your goal for this class?" Now, most of the students said it was to get a good grade, pass the class or something similar, but for some reason, Whitney said something entirely different. She said that her goal was to make just one good friend.

While most of the students sat in silence, one student came to Whitney and held out his hand and introduced himself. He asked if she would be his friend. The whole room was silent—all eyes focused on Whitney and the hand extended just in front of her. She smiled and stretched her hand out to take his and a friendship was formed. It was a friendship that lasted all through college. It was a friendship that turned into a romance. It was a friendship that brought two people together in marriage.

Whitney learned the power of asking for what she wanted, being honest and taking action.

Questions

(1) What kind of person is Whitney? What is her problem?

She was a bit shy and reserved. She wanted to make some real friends to share secrets and laugh with.

(2) Is Whitney's goal for her class unexpected? Why or why not?

Yes. Because her goal for her class was quite unique, entirely different from all the other pupils'.

2. Fill in the form and discuss the writing skills with your partner.

Theme	Friendship
Purpose	*To tell readers that it is important to reach out for a true friend*

(Continued on the next page)

Writing skills	*Suspense and contrast*
Examples	***Suspense:*** *The first week of classes, one thing that changed Whitney's life forever.* ***Contrast:*** *Now, most of the students said it was to get a good grade, pass the class or something similar, but for some reason, Whitney said something entirely different. She said that her goal was to make just one good friend.* *While most of the students sat in silence, one student came to Whitney and held out his hand and introduced himself.*

Step 2   Choose a topic.

1. Think of your topic, purpose of writing and the basic elements of the story and fill in the table.

Teaching Notes

通过表格填写和同伴讨论引导学生围绕主题 "Friendship" 构思自己的作文,确定文章的主题和大致框架结构。如果学生有困难,教师可以通过提问启发学生。

Example

Theme	Friendship
Topic	*An unexpected friendship*
Purpose (why do you choose this topic)	*To tell readers that friendship sometimes starts from a kind action unexpectedly*
Setting (when & where)	*School campus (Scene 1)*
	School hall (Scene 2)
Person	The Third Person
Characters (who will be in the story)	*Jason and Nancy (strangers at first and friends later)*
Tense	*Mainly past tense*

2. Discuss it with your partner and ask him/her whether it sounds good or interesting.

Step 3　Develop it into an outline and share it with your peers.

Fill in the table to collect more details using the strategies of suspense and contrast.

Teaching Notes

通过本活动引导学生在写初稿前收集材料信息，注意范文中的写作技巧：设置悬念和对比描写，为写初稿做好铺垫。

Example

Suspense	More details (using contrast)
Suspense1 *One day, Jason was walking home from school. He didn't expect what happened later would change his life forever.* *Suspense 2* *Jason gave a speech …*	Beginning: *Jason was on his way home as usual; alone* Middle: *a group of kids ran towards him* *he was knocked out* *his books went out of his arms* *his glasses went flying* *Nancy came and helped him* Ending: *at the graduation ceremony* *Jason told the story of the first day* *Jason smiled at Nancy*

Drafting and Revising

Step 4　Complete your first draft.

Complete the first draft by further expanding the outline.

Teaching Notes

要求学生根据表格列出文章内容，并强调注意运用设置悬念和对比描写的写作手法。

The first draft

Topic: *The Power of Friendship*

Beginning: (Setting, main characters)

　　One day, Jason was walking home alone from school as usual. He didn't expect that the things which happened later would change his life forever.

Middle: (Events; suspense, contrast)

As he was walking, a group of kids ran towards him, knocking all his books out of his arms and tripping him so he fell into the dirt. His glasses went flying. Jason looked up and there was terrible sadness in his eyes. Instead of rushing to apologize, those kids stood around mocking the "nerd" coldly. Unlike those guys, Nancy came and helped him find his glasses. He looked at her and said thanks. There was a big smile on his face. It was one of those smiles that showed real gratitude. They have become friends since that day.

Time flied, and soon came the graduation ceremony. Jason was the student who was honored to deliver a speech, and to Nancy's surprise, he told the story of the first day they met. He had planned to kill himself over the weekend. He looked hard at Nancy and gave her a little smile. "Thankfully, I was saved. My friend saved me," he added.

Ending: (Reflections)

Never underestimate the power of our actions. With one small gesture we can change a person's life. For better or for worse, we are in each other's lives to impact one another in some way.

Step 5   Self-check and peer check.

Revise your first draft using the questions below as a guide.

> **Teaching Notes**
>
> 要求学生根据检查列表中的问题修改习作,并对同伴的作文提出修改意见。

Checklist

- ☐ Do I use suspense at the beginning of the story to hook readers?
- ☐ Do I give enough details in the story?
- ☐ Do I use contrast to highlight the difference before and after?
- ☐ Do I give my reflections to deepen the meaning of the story?

The improved version

The Power of Friendship

One day, Jason was walking home from school as usual. He didn't expect that the things which happened later would change his life forever.

When he got to the street corner, a group of kids ran towards him, knocking all his books out of his arms and tripping him so he fell into the dirt and his glasses went flying. Instead of making an apology, those kids stood around mocking the "nerd" coldly. ~~Unlike those guys, Nancy came and helped him find his glasses.~~ *Just as Jason crawled around looking for his glasses, Nancy came over to him and said, "They really should be punished."* ① He looked at her and said thanks. There was a big smile on his face. It was one of those smiles that showed real gratitude. ~~They have become friends since that day.~~ *And the gratitude gradually grew into friendship.* ②

Time flied, and soon came the graduation ceremony. Jason stood on the stage, starting to deliver a speech. To Nancy's surprise, *Jason turned his face slightly towards her and said:"Being a friend to someone is the best gift you can give them. I am going to tell you a story ..."* ③ He told the story of the first day they met. He looked hard at Nancy and gave her a little smile. "Thankfully, I was saved. My friend saved me," he added.

Never underestimate the power of our actions. With one small gesture we can change a person's life. For better or for worse, we are in each other's lives to impact one another in some way. *Friends can make us fly high while enemies just make us cry.* ④

修改说明:

① 增加对话和细节描写,丰富故事情节。

② 改写句子,gratitude 和 friendship 两个词揭示了俩人关系的变化,是对文章开头悬念的解释。

③ 插入动作和对话,引出下文。

④ 使用对比句式表述感悟,凸显主题。

Editing and Proofreading

Step 6   Once you have completed your revising, improve the language of your essay and make sure that there are no mistakes in punctuation, capitalization, spelling and grammar. Then write a neat final copy to share.

Model essay

One day, as Jason was walking home from school as usual, he didn't expect that what was about to happen would change his life forever.

When he got to the street corner, a group of kids ran toward him, knocking his books out of his hands, tripping him up. Jason fell into the dirt and his glasses were sent flying. Instead of saying sorry, the kids stood around mocking him, calling him a "nerd". Just as Jason was crawling around looking for his glasses, Nancy came over.

"They really should be punished," she said. Jason looked at her.

"Thanks," he replied, with a big smile on his face. It was one of those smiles that showed real gratitude. And that gratitude gradually grew into friendship.

Time flew by and graduation day arrived. Jason climbed up on the stage, and started to deliver his speech. Turning towards her, Jason said that friendship was the best gift we could give someone. Then, to Nancy's surprise, he went on to tell everyone the story of how they met. He smiled at Nancy and finished with:

"Thankfully, I was saved. My friend saved me."

We should never underestimate the power of our actions. With one small gesture we can change a person's life. For better or for worse, we are in each other's lives and impact upon one another in some way. Friends can make us fly high while enemies just make us cry.

三、说明文写作教学实践（Practice on Expository Writing）

Writing Task　Write an expository passage defining a "gap year". [①]

Teaching Focus

♦ Use a logical definition

♦ Use details or examples to make the definition clear

Prewriting

Step 1　Read the passage. Find out the logical definition of hibernation and the ways to define hibernation. Then complete the table.

Teaching Notes

通过阅读文本并完成表格填写，引导学生从具体案例中理解和感悟用下定义的方法进行说明文写作的要点，以及如何通过举例等方法对所定义的概念及其特点作进一步说明。

The Mystery of Hibernation

What do bears, bats and frogs have in common? They all hibernate. Hibernation is a state often compared to sleep. It usually occurs in winter, when a creature does not move for weeks or months continuously. Creatures hibernate to survive the cold weather and the absence of food.

A typical example of a hibernating creature is the bat. When winter comes, bats find a safe place in a cave. Looking like they are dead, they hang upside down. Their pulse and breathing rates greatly slow down. Their body temperatures drop as well. These things help them save energy during long winters when it is difficult to find food.

Frogs, like many amphibians, also hibernate when it gets cold. After

---

① 本案例作者为上海市七宝中学黄岳辉。

digging deep into the mud at the bottom of a pond, they do not stir again until it is warm. During hibernation, they breathe through their skins, not their mouths.

Another hibernating creature is the bear. In contrast to other creatures, hibernating bears do not appear as though they are dead, but seem as though they are very sleepy. If they are disturbed during hibernation, they can get up very quickly. While hibernating, bears stay in their dens, which are filled with leaves to make their stay more comfortable and warmer. In spring, having awakened, they leave their dens, thin and hungry.

Term defined	*hibernation*
Class	*a state of sleep*
Characteristics	*• usually occurring in winter* *• a creature not moving for weeks or months continuously* *• creatures to survive the cold weather and absence of food*
Logical definition	*Hibernation is a state of sleep which usually occurs in winter when a creature does no move for weeks or months continuously to survive the cold weather and the absence of food.*
Way to define it	*Use examples to provide additional information to make the definition and the characteristics of hibernation clearer to readers.*

Step 2 Brainstorming: Discuss the following question with your partners.

If you want to write an expository passage about a "gap year", what comes into your mind? When necessary, you may consult the dictionary or search on the Internet. Make a list.

Teaching Notes

通过有关"gap year"的"头脑风暴"活动激活学生思路。教师需根据学生情况,如有必要可让学生查阅有关"gap year"的定义和相关信息。

(1)_____   (2)_____
(3)_____ Gap year (4)_____
...   ...

Example

(1) *What is a gap year?*

(2) *How did the gap year come into being?*

(3) *What do students usually do during the gap year?*

(4) *What benefits does the gap year bring to students?*

...

Drafting and Revising

Step 3　Look over the list you've made and choose the items you are going to write about.

Teaching Notes

　　本活动旨在帮助学生在"头脑风暴"的基础上根据写作要点选择写作内容并列出初步框架结构,然后完成初稿。

Ask yourself the following questions when writing the first draft.

- What is the definition of a gap year?
- What are the characteristics of a gap year?
- What details or examples can I use to make it clear?

Example

Definition	*A gap year is a year before going to college or university after high school.*
Characteristics	*non-academic courses, such as learning a trade, doing volunteer work, travelling, doing sports ...*
Details	● *Experience different cultures and broad one's horizons* ● *Develop one's independence and sense of responsibility* ● *Get a clear understanding of one's own strengths and weaknesses* *...*

The first draft

　　Gap year is becoming increasingly popular in western countries. During this time students mainly engage in non-academic courses, such as learning a trade, volunteer work, travel, sports and more.

Gap years are considered as a great way for students to learn about the world and foster a great deal of responsibility prior to university life. For example, most gap year students in America take the chance to travel to or work in different cities at home and even abroad, where they experience various cultures and interesting lessons about the world. This helps them to work out who they are and what they are for.

I am in favour of the proposal that the gap year practice should be carried in China because it is a good chance for us students to learn to overcome difficulties and get along well in the real world. Also, the experience will help a lot in cultivating independence.

Step 4   Self-check and peer check.

Revise your first draft using the questions below as a guide.

> **Teaching Notes**
>
> 以问题形式提供检查列表，为学生提供修改标准。

Checklist

☐ Have I presented a clear definition of the gap year at the beginning?

☐ Have I provided detailed information about the characteristics of the gap year to make it clearer?

The improved version

A gap year, *commonly a year before going to college or university after high school,* ① is becoming increasingly popular in western countries. During this time students mainly engage in non-academic courses, such as learning a trade, volunteer work, travel, sports and more.

Gap years are considered as a great way for students to learn about the world and foster a great deal of responsibility prior to university life. For example, most gap year students in America take the chance to travel to or work in different cities at home and even abroad, where they experience various cultures and interesting lessons about the world. This helps them to work out who they are and what they are for.

Gap year students may face challenges, frustrations and failures. They have to learn how to overcome these difficulties and get along well in the real world. This process isn't always easy, but it is an important part of growing up for them to cultivate their independence. ②

> 修改说明：
> ① 对"gap year"作清晰完整的定义。
> ② 用客观的语言，在结尾重申"gap year"的重要性和积极意义。

Editing and Proofreading

Step 5   Once you have completed your revising, improve the language of your essay and make sure that there are no mistakes in punctuation, capitalization, spelling and grammar. Then write a neat final copy to share.

Model essay

The practice of taking a gap year, a year taken out of studies before going to college or university, is becoming increasingly popular in Western countries. During this time students mainly travel, try learning a trade, or even do some volunteer work at home or overseas.

Gap years are considered as a great way for students to learn about the world; it gives them the chances to learn responsibility prior to university life. For example, most gap year students in America go to different cities both at home and abroad, where they experience differing cultures and are able to learn a great deal about the world in a non-academic setting. This helps them to work out who they are and what they want out of life.

During the experience, gap year students may have to deal with many challenges, frustrations and even failures. They have to learn how to overcome these difficulties and survive in the real world. It's not always easy, but it's an important part of growing up and becoming more independent.

四、议论文写作教学实践（Practice on Argumentative Writing）

Writing Task 某大学最近决定改变奖学金颁发制度，将奖学金金额降为一元，并将多余款项用于资助海外交流项目，此决定在大学生中引发热议。你认为这所大学的做法可取吗？请阐述你的观点。①

Teaching Focus

◇ Make a clear statement of your viewpoint

◇ Give a logical analysis of the issue

◇ Use adequate evidence

Prewriting

Teaching Notes

通过阅读范文，引导学生关注话题讨论类议论文写作的要点：描述现象或话题，清晰地表达观点并用充分的论据进行论证。

Step 1　Read the sample passage.

Read the passage and answer the questions below.

With the curtains just down on the Rio Olympics, whether Shanghai should bid for the 2028 Summer Olympics has aroused wide public concern. An estimated 70 percent of the netizens on Sina Micro Blog are in favour of Shanghai making the move, and I am one of them. Needless to say, staging the 2028 Summer Olympics is of considerable significance to the host city.

---

① 本案例作者为上海市青浦高级中学陆永梅。

In the first place, Summer Olympics have always been among the most high-profiled international events. The host city of it will attract massive international attention, which serves as a golden opportunity to help the city promote its image on the international stage. Additionally, in the process of the Olympics, numerous domestic and foreign visitors will flood into the city, which affords an ideal opportunity to boost the city's tourism. It contributes to the development of the city's economy and is regarded as a good solution to relieving the city's unemployment pressure. Moreover, with worldwide focus on the city, her unique charm, diverse cultures and fine tradition open its door to the whole world, which serves as an excellent opportunity to foster the city's brand-new image.

With the experience accumulated in staging the 2010 World Expo successfully, I am convinced that Shanghai has the capacity to take on the challenge and present the world with a great success of the Olympics. In the meantime, Shanghai grasps the opportunities to move to the next stage financially, socially and culturally. As a Shanghainese, I can't wait to play my part in the Olympics.

Questions

(1) What issue does the writer talk about?

Whether Shanghai should bid for the 2028 Summer Olympics.

(2) What is the writer's opinion?

The writer is strongly in favour of Shanghai bidding for the Games.

(3) How does the writer support his opinion?

The writer supports his opinion by using facts and reasoning.

Step 2　Discuss the following questions.

(1) What is the purpose of a scholarship?

To motivate students to achieve academic excellence/to help relieve students' financial

Teaching Notes

　　教师通过问题引发学生讨论奖学金设定和海外交流项目的目的，以及改变奖学金可能带来的后果和影响，帮助学生确定观点，为之后的写作准备。

burden. ...

(2) What is the purpose of exchange programmes?

To broaden students' horizons/to enhance cultural exchange. ...

(3) What will be the possible result if the scholarship is reduced to one yuan?

The students' passion for study may be dampened. ...

Step 3   Decide your opinion and make an outline.

1. State your opinion and list supporting details.

> ### Teaching Notes
> 通过完成写作提纲，引导学生尝试围绕话题选择立场，陈述观点，罗列出支持的论据，并初步形成论证思路。

Example

My opinion: *I will definitely say no to the changes in scholarship policy made in the University.*

Supporting detail 1: *The scholarship can be used to help relieve the financial burden of some students.*

Supporting detail 2: *Money can be used to motivate students to achieve academic excellence.*

Supporting detail 3: *China is not the only country that awards scholarships to motivate students' academic excellence.*

2. Discuss a student's outline, find out the problem(s) and improve it.

My opinion: The scholarship policy should not be changed in the university.

Supporting detail 1: The scholarship can be used to help relieve the financial burden of some students.

Supporting detail 2: The scholarship is intended to encourage students to achieve academic excellence.（奖学金与金钱不能混为一谈）

Supporting detail 3: The scholarship can benefit more students than the fund for overseas exchange programmes.（将奖学金与海外交流项目的得益人群比较）

Drafting and Revising

Step 4   Complete your first draft.

The first draft

The recent news that a prestigious university in China decided to reduce the scholarship awards to only one yuan was a hot topic on the web.

Different people have different attitudes towards the issue. Some students feel it upset to open the envelope containing one yuan like beggars in the street. However, other students hold an opposite opinion.

In my opinion, the change made by the university was improper because the one-yuan scholarship might dampen the enthusiasm of hard-working college students. Scholarship is intended to help relieve the financial burden of some students from poor families. Moreover, many universities in the world award scholarships to the students with outstanding academic performance. Why not follow their steps? Every change made is a double-edged sword. The change made by the university can strengthen the overseas exchange programme, but it will be beneficial to fewer students.

Step 5   Self-check and peer check.

Revise your first draft using the questions below as a guide.

Checklist

☐ Do I give a clear opinion in my thesis statement?

☐ Do I give at least two supporting points?

☐ Are the points presented in a logical way?

☐ Do I use enough details to support my points?

☐ Do I emphasize my opinion in the ending?

The improved version

The recent news that a prestigious university in China decided to reduce the scholarship awards to only one yuan so as to use the extra money to sponsor overseas exchange programme has been a hot topic on the web. Students in most colleges feel upset about the change. A different voice has made itself heard. *In my opinion, it is obviously a bad move*. ①

First, ② the scholarship is intended to motivate students positively and encourage them to achieve academic excellence. The reason why many world top universities keep the scholarships and never reduce them is that they really understand the value of scholarship—it is an honour for the students.

Second, ② it can help relieve the financial burden of some students and supports them to complete their studies.

Last but not least, ② scholarship can benefit more students while the overseas exchange programme involves fewer.

In brief, the school authority should rethink its one yuan scholarship policy before it dampens the enthusiasm of those diligent students. ③

> 修改说明：
> ① 首段在描述现象后清晰地表明自己的观点。
> ② 中间段依次用三个论据支撑自己的观点，并用表示顺序的连接词，使论据的呈现更有层次感。
> ③ 增加了结尾段，使文章首尾呼应，更有说服力。

Editing and Proofreading

Step 6 Once you have completed your revising, improve the language of your essay and make sure that there are no mistakes in punctuation, capitalization, spelling and grammar. Then write a neat final copy to share.

Model essay

The recent news that a prestigious university in China has decided to reduce the scholarship awards to only one yuan, in order to use the extra money for sponsoring an overseas exchange programme has been a hot topic on the web. Students in most colleges feel upset about the change. In my opinion, it is obviously a bad move.

First, the scholarship is intended to motivate students positively and encourage them to achieve academic excellence. The reason why many top universities in the world retain scholarships is that they really understand their value. It is an honour for the students.

Second, it can help relieve the financial burden of some students and support them to complete their studies.

Last but not least, scholarships can benefit more students, while the overseas exchange programme involves fewer students.

In brief, the university authority should rethink its one yuan scholarship policy before it dampens the enthusiasm of those diligent students.

五、应用文写作教学实践（Practice on Practical Writing）

Writing Task　Write a letter of complaint.[①]

Teaching Focus

◇ State the writing purpose and the problem clearly

◇ Write the complaint letter with a proper structure

◇ Use appropriate language

Prewriting

Step 1　Read the sample letters.

Read two sample letters and answer the questions.

> **Teaching Notes**
>
> 　　通过阅读两篇范文并回答问题，帮助学生理解投诉信的框架结构以及各段落承担的作用，明确写信对象（即：读者）和写信目的。

① 本案例作者为上海市晋元高级中学汤晓华。

Letter 1

Dear Manager,

I write this letter to place a complaint against the bad delivery service of your company.

The Apple iPad I ordered from your company arrived yesterday. I am sorry to find that the packing case was broken and that the home button of the device was struck and could not work. What's more, there were some scratches on the surface of the camera. Since there was such damage to the goods, I decided to file a complaint against the delivery service.

Would you let me know whether I should return the iPad for a replacement or if I can get refunded? I will hold on to this iPad until I hear from you. I would like to have this matter settled by December 18, or I will appeal to the press.

Sincerely yours,

Pool George

Letter 2

To whom it may concern,

I am writing to express my dissatisfaction with the service in your restaurant.

On November 26th, I dined with some friends at your restaurant. When we were there, no waitress or waiter actively served us. When we were about to order, they again ignored us, having small talk. When knowing we only ordered some set dinners, not the Thanksgiving turkey, the waitress called Jessie was rather arrogant and aggressive.

So I really wish that you could pay more attention to your staff training and would never allow such a thing to happen again. Thank you for your time and consideration.

Yours sincerely,

Raymond

Questions

(1) Who wrote the letters?

Letter 1: Pool George; Letter 2: Raymond.

(2) Who are the letters intended for?

Letter 1: the manager; Letter 2: anyone in charge of the restaurant.

(3) Why did they write the letters?

To complain about the goods or the service they have got.

(4) What does each paragraph tell us?

Para. 1 *states the problem*.

Para. 2 *provides more information*.

Para. 3 *is about the appeal*.

Step 2　Trial run.

Pair work: Read the letter below and find out the problems in it.

> *Teaching Notes*
>
> 本活动目的在于引导学生通过阅读一篇投诉信草稿,发现该封投诉信在框架结构、语言使用中的问题,帮助他们理解和感悟投诉信写作应该注意的问题。

Hi, buddy,

Because of the very very wet floor, I slipped like a stupid turtle. But the staff laughed at me, doing nothing at all and walked away.

So now I write the letter with my heart broken to tell a story about a sad thing that many many people saw last Friday, which made me a fool.

I promise I would never allow my friends to shop at your place but I hope you can improve the sense of responsibility to prevent the recurrence of similar accidents. Besides, I need an apology, or else.

Yours poorly,

Jinx

Problems in the letter

Hi, buddy, ···· | Salutation: The language is informal and not serious. |

Because of the very very wet floor, I slipped like a stupid turtle. But the staff laughed at me, doing nothing at all and walked away. ····

| Para. 1: The problem is not clearly stated and the language is inappropriate. |

So now I write the letter with my heart broken to tell a story about a sad thing that many many people saw last Friday, which made me a fool. ····

| Para. 2: The details are not stated in a logical and factual way. |

I promise I would never allow my friends to shop at your place but I hope you can improve the sense of responsibility to prevent the recurrence of similar accidents. Besides, I need an apology, or else. ····

| Para. 3: The appeal is not reasonable and practical. |

Yours poorly,

Jinx

| Signature: The tone is not serious or businesslike. |

Step 3　Discuss the tips with your partner and then complete the table below. ····

Teaching Notes

学生通过讨论归纳出书写投诉信必须注意的要点问题，为后续写作奠定基础。必要时，教师可给予提示和帮助。

Tips on how to write a letter of complaint

Aspect	Content	Tips
Structure	purpose & problem	*clearly & directly stated*
	information	*factual, logically organized*
	appeal	*reasonable, practical*
Language	*formal, appropriate*	
Tone	*serious, businesslike*	

Drafting and Revising

Writing Task Suppose a friend of yours had a heavy fall on the wet floor when shopping in the supermarket. The store staff didn't offer any help. Write a letter of complaint to the manager of the supermarket about the experience of your friend.

Step 4 **Write the first paragraph of the letter. Then discuss in groups each other's first draft, asking yourself the following questions.**

> **Teaching Notes**
>
> 以首段的写作为例,引导学生依据投诉信每一部分的内容要求进行写作。先让学生自己写,然后进行小组讨论,通过自我修正和相互批改落实投诉信首段的写作要点: 开门见山说明问题、语言要精练、语气要不卑不亢。

- Is the purpose/reason of my letter clearly explained?
- Is the problem stated directly and clearly?
- Does it sound like the beginning of a formal letter?

Example

I *hate to interrupt you, but I have to*（口语化,随意）because I *suffered a lot yesterday in your supermarket.*（太笼统,投诉问题不清楚）

The improved version

I'm writing to file a complaint about the shopping environment and the poor service in your supermarket.

Step 5 **Finish the letter of complaint by yourself. Then revise it according to the checklist.**

> **Teaching Notes**
>
> 在此环节应给予学生充分的时间,引导学生按照检查列表写作,并进行自我修正。也可以通过同伴互评来改进初稿。提醒学生在修改时,要关注语言的适切性和规范性。

Checklist

☐ Is the complaint stated clearly and directly?

☐ Is the information factual and relevant?

☐ Is the suggestion reasonable and practical?

☐ Is the language appropriate and formal?

☐ Is the tone serious and businesslike?

The first draft

June 22nd, 2016

Dear Manager,

I'm writing to file a complaint about the shopping environment and the poor service in your supermarket.

I was shopping in your supermarket several days ago. But I fell down because of a pool of water on the floor. Your staff blamed me for the fall and didn't come to my help at all, which hurt me so much.

I demand that you should pay me a 3,000 for the accident and dismiss the staff immediately, otherwise I will do something to teach you a lesson. Wait for your reply.

Sincerely yours,

John Houston

The improved version

June 22nd, 2016

Dear Manager,

I am writing the letter to make a complaint about the environment and service of your supermarket.

I was shopping in your supermarket *on June, 18* ① . There was a pool of water on the floor in your supermarket, *but no sign*

修改说明：

① 事实细节和问题要准确 说明。

② 提出的建议要合情合理。

③ 语言表达应恰当，态度要 有礼有节。

was put there to warn the customers to be cautious ① . Not having noticed it, I fell badly. *Instead of helping me up, the staff laughed at me and blamed me for it.* ①

I file the complaint to *suggest that you should provide a safe and pleasant shopping environment for the customers and strengthen the sense of responsibility of your staff to prevent the recurrence of similar accidents* ② . *Thank you for your time and consideration.* ③

Sincerely yours,

John Houston

Editing and Proofreading

Step 6   Once you have completed the revising, use the following checklist as a guide for proper formatting and conventions. Then write a neat final copy to share.

Teaching Notes

　　本活动旨在让学生在对投诉信的格式和语言按照要求修改之后,继续关注某些细节,如拼写、标点、时态,等等。

Editing Checklist

☐ Does my letter follow the structure of a complaint letter?

☐ Have I checked for punctuation and capitalization?

☐ Have I checked for spelling errors?

☐ Have I used correct tenses?

☐ Have I used appropriate language?

Model essay

Dear Manager,

　　I am writing to complain about two issues which I am very concerned about:

both the environment and the standard of service I experienced while visiting your supermarket.

On 18 June, while I was shopping in your supermarket, there was a pool of water on the floor, but without any signage warning customers to be cautious. Not having noticed it, I fell badly and injured myself. Instead of helping me up, the staff laughed at me and blamed me for it.

I would like your assurance that you will provide a safe and pleasant shopping environment for customers, and that your staff will receive better training to prevent the recurrence of similar accidents. Thank you for your time and consideration.

Sincerely yours,

John Houston

参 考 文 献

［1］布兰顿.中学生英语写作新视野［M］.张文明译注.上海：上海教育出版社，2015.

［2］陈立平.实用英语应用文写作［M］.北京：金盾出版社，2014.

［3］丁往道,吴冰,钟美荪.英语写作手册［M］.北京:外语教学与研究出版社，2009.

［4］傅似逸.英语写作：应用文写作［M］.北京：北京大学出版社，2015.

［5］韩金龙.英语写作教学——过程体裁教学法［J］.外语界，2001，4.

［6］何亚男，金怡，张育青，等.高中英语写作教学设计［M］.上海：上海教育出版社，2017.

［7］兰良平，韩刚.英语写作教学—课堂互动性交流视角［M］.北京：外语教学与研究出版社，2014.

［8］刘海平.写作教程［M］.上海：上海外语教育出版社，2008.

［9］鲁瑛.英语应用文写作教程［M］.北京：对外经济贸易大学出版社，2012.

［10］潘宝艳.中学生英语日记精品［M］.北京：北京工业大学出版社，2002.

［11］秦显贵.英语日记大全（高中生）［M］.北京：华文出版社，2007.

［12］唐文洁，李萍.名校名师：高考英语作文全攻略［M］.上海：上海教育出版社，2012.

［13］田樱花.星级英语写作方法与技巧（高中）［M］.上海：百家出版社，2007.

［14］吴锦，张在新.英语写作教学法新探——论写前阶段的可行性［J］.外语教学与研究，2000，32（3）：213-218.

［15］徐强.“写信”在任务型教学评估中的设计问题——以高考英语上海卷为例［J］.中小学英语教学与研究，2012，268（6）：70-72.

［16］亚历山大，何其莘.新概念英语2：实践与进步［M］.北京：外语教学与

研究出版社，1997.

［17］亚历山大，何其莘.新概念英语3：培养技能［M］.北京：外语教学与研究出版社，1997.

［18］杨朝春.英语说明文读写教程［M］.北京：清华大学出版社，2013.

［19］中华人民共和国教育部.普通高中英语课程标准（2017年版2020年修订）［M］.北京：人民教育出版社，2020.

［20］Brookes A, Grundy P. Beginning to Write［M］. Cambridge: Cambridge University Press, 1999.

［21］Campbell C. Teaching Second Language Writing: Interacting with Text［M］. Beijing: Foreign Language Teaching Press, 2009.

［22］Chandrasegaran A. Intervening to Help in the Writing Process［M］. Beijing: People's Education Press, 2007.

［23］Doyle A. Job Application Letter Sample［R/OL］.［2016−05−21］. https://www.thebalance.com/job-application-letter-sample-2062548.

［24］Evans V. Successful Writing［M］. London: Express Publishing, 2000.

［25］Flower L, Hayes J R. A Cognitive Process Theory of Writing［J］. College Composition and Communication, 1981.

［26］Glencoe Writer's Choice: Grammar and Composition［M］. New York: McGraw-Hill Education, 2001.

［27］Glenn C. Making Sense: A Real-World Rhetorical Reader (Second ed)［M］. Boston: Bedford/St. Martin's, 2005.

［28］Hedge T. Teaching and Learning in the Language Classroom［M］. Shanghai: Shanghai Foreign Language Education Press, 2002.

［29］Hogue A. Longman Academic Writing Series［M］. London: Pearson Education, Inc.

［30］How to Organize a School Prom or Formal［R/OL］.［2015−07−10］. http://hubpages.com/education/How-to-Organize-a-School-Prom-or-Formal.

［31］How to Write a Letter of Application for a Job［EB/OL］.［2016−05−21］. http://www.wikihow.com/Write-a-Letter-of-Application-for-a-Job.

［32］How to Write to a Pen Pal for the First Time［EB/OL］.［2016−10−24］. http://www.wikihow.com/Write-to-a-Pen-Pal-for-the-First-Time.

［33］ Kemper D, Sebranek P, Meyer V. Write Source—A Book for Writing, Thinking and Learning［M］. GREAT SOURCE, 2005.

［34］ Kemper D, Sebranek P, Meyer V. Write Source［M］. Boston: Houghton Mifflin Harcourt: 2012.

［35］ Kemper D, Sebranek P, Meyer V. Write Source［M］. Boston: Houghton Mifflin Harcourt, 2004.

［36］ Raimes A. Techniques in Teaching Writing［M］. Oxford: Oxford University Press, 1983.

［37］ Reynolds J. Cambridge Checkpoint 1［M］. London: Hodder Education Press, 2011.

［38］ Rumisek L A, Zemach D E. Academic Writing: From Paragraph to Essay［M］. London: Macmillan Education, 2005.

［39］ Weigle S C. Assessing Writing［M］. Cambridge: Cambridge University Press, 2002.

［40］ Students Should Not Be Allowed to Use Cell Phones at School［R/OL］.［2016-05-21］. https://academichelp.net/samples/academics/essays/persuasive/cell-phones-at-school.html.

［41］ Why Plastic Surgery is Acceptable［R/OL］.［2016-05-21］. https://academichelp.net/samples/academics/essays/persuasive/plastic-surgery-accept.html.

［42］ Why Teens Should Not Be Allowed to Play Violent Video Games［R/OL］.［2016-05-21］. https://academichelp.net/samples/academics/essays/persuasive/violent-games. html.

网站资源：

［1］ http://journalism.about.com

［2］ http://www.primaryresources.co.uk/english/englishD10.htm

［3］ http://www.scholastic.com

［4］ http://www.twinkl.co.uk/resources/ks2-non-fiction-persuasive-writing

［5］ https://www.tes.com/teaching-resources